Eastern Civilization from a Catholic Viewpoint: Foundational Thought and Beliefs

Fr. Peter Samuel Kucer, MSA

En Route Books & Media, LLC
St. Louis, MO, USA

En Route Books and Media, LLC
5705 Rhodes Avenue
St. Louis, MO 63109

Cover credit: TJ Burdick

Library of Congress Control Number: 2017956390

Copyright © 2019 Peter Samuel Kucer

ISBN-10: 0-9994704-5-0
ISBN-13: 978-0-9994704-5-9

No part of this booklet may be reproduced, stored in a retrieval system, or transmitted in any form, or by any means, electronic, mechanical, photocopying, or otherwise, without the prior written permission of the author.

DEDICATION

In memory of my mother, Roberta Kucer, who instilled in me a love of study and a love of her people, the chosen people.

In addition, I dedicate this book to the members of my community, the Missionaries of the Holy Apostles.

ACKNOWLEDGMENTS

I would particularly like to acknowledge Fr. Isaac Martinez, MSA, former General of the Missionaries of the Holy Apostles, who gave me permission to publish, and Bishop Christian Rodembourg, MSA, who as the first MSA to be ordained a bishop brought our MSA charism into a deeper ecclesial dimension by assuming the office of bishop the year this book was published. Special thanks to Dr. Sebastian Mahfood, OP, president of En Route Books and Media, for publishing this work.

CONTENTS

Chapter 1: Man and Civilization 1
Man 2
Pre-historic Eras 4
Civilization: Strengths and Weaknesses 9
Quiz 1 for Chapter 1 15

Chapter 2: Ancient China and India 17
The Shang Dynasty 18
The Zhou Dynasty 22
Yijing (I Ching) 24
Vedas 25
Upanishads (*Upaniṣads*) 27
Uddalaka 32
Quiz 2 for Chapter 2 33

Chapter 3: Vedanta Hinduism 37
Shankara and Vedanta Absolute Monism or non-Dualism . 38
Ramanuja and Vedanta Qualified non-Dualism 39
Madhva and Vedanta Dualism 42
Quiz 3 for Chapter 3 46

Chapter 4: Yoga Hinduism 49
Samkhya 50
Patanjali: Founder of Yoga 52
Hatha Yoga 55
Quiz 4 for Chapter 4 59

Chapter 5: Indian Extreme Pluralism and Persian (Iranian) Dualism 63
Jainism and Pluralism 63
Zoroastrianism 67
Mani and Manichaeism 71
Quiz 5 for Chapter 5 74

Chapter 6: Hindu Gods - Monotheism and Pantheism 77
Hindu Mythology 80
A Few Popular Hindu Gods 82
Quiz 6 for Chapter 6 90

Chapter 7: Buddha 93
Buddha 93
Four Noble Truths 98
Eight Fold Path 100
Moral Precepts: Five, Eight, and Ten 101
Quiz 7 for Chapter 7 104

Chapter 8: Mahayana, Theravada and Tibetan Buddhism 107
Origin of Buddhist Traditions 110
Theravada Buddhism 112
Mahayana Buddhism 115
Tibetan Buddhism 128
Quiz 8 for Chapter 8 132

Chapter 9: Laozi, Daoism and Chinese Buddhism 135
Daoism 135
Chan Buddhism 145
Han-shan (Cold Mountain) 148
Zen Buddhism 151
Quiz 9 for Chapter 9 156

Chapter 10: Confucius and Confucianism 159
Confucius 160
Family 162
Scholarship 164
Conformity 166
Action and Civic Duty 168
Quiz 10 for Chapter 10 169

Chapter 11: Confucian Schools and Reconciliation with Daoism 171
Mencius and Human Nature 172
Xunzi and Human Nature 175
Confucianism: Mencius and Daoism 177
Quiz 11 for Chapter 11 180

Chapter 12: Legalism 183
Lord Shang and Legalism 184
Han Feizi and Confucian Virtue 189
Quiz 12 for Chapter 12 196

Chapter 1: Man and Civilization

Introduction

In this chapter we will focus on two fundamental realities that are foundational to this course, man and civilization. We will begin with a Catholic concept of what, or, more properly, who man is. Then we will take a critical look at the discoveries of paleo-anthropology, coming from two Greek words meaning the science of ancient men. In doing this, the following pre-historic ages will be introduced: Paleolithic, Neolithic, Bronze Age, and Iron Age. Since the Iron Age is generally considered the last era of pre-history, before human history was recorded by writing, we will then shift our attention to the study of civilization.

The English word civilization is based on the Latin word *civis*. A *civis* was considered someone who lived in a city, *civitas*. The study of civilization, therefore, means literally the study of people living in community, specifically cities. Cities and their civilizations are born, decline, and, sometimes, regenerate. Explanations as to why this occurs greatly vary.[1]

Man

Knowing who we are is essential when studying Eastern civilization from a Catholic perspective. According to official Catholic teaching, man is not simply different in degree from animals. Rather, we are different in kind. In other words, we are not merely highly evolved animals. Our ability to reason is not only due to a slow process of evolution in which consciousness gradually developed, but also to our having been created in the image and likeness of God. This does not mean, however, that all evolutionary theories are necessarily incompatible with Catholic belief.

As far back as the 1950s, Pope Pius XII in his encyclical letter *Humani Generis* affirmed that some evolutionary theories are not contrary to Catholic teaching as long as it is believed that at one point in time God infused a rational soul capable of eternal and joyful communion with him into the first man and first woman.

Pope Pius XII *Humani Generis*

For these reasons the Teaching Authority of the

---

[1] This chapter is a slight adaptation of chapter one from my book *Western Civilization from Pre-historical Times to the Protestant Reformation* (En Route Books and Media, 2019).

Church does not forbid that, in conformity with the present state of human sciences and sacred theology, research and discussions, on the part of men experienced in both fields, take place with regard to the doctrine of evolution, in as far as it inquires into the origin of the human body as coming from pre-existent and living matter - for the Catholic faith obliges us to hold that souls are immediately created by God. However, this must be done in such a way that the reasons for both opinions, that is, those favorable and those unfavorable to evolution, be weighed and judged with the necessary seriousness, moderation and measure, and provided that all are prepared to submit to the judgment of the Church, to whom Christ has given the mission of interpreting authentically the Sacred Scriptures and of defending the dogmas of faith.[2]

Similarly, Pope Saint John Paul II stated in a General Audience of April 16th, 1986, that:

It can therefore be said that, from the viewpoint of the doctrine of the faith, there are no difficulties in explaining the origin of man in regard to the body, by means of the theory of evolution. But it must be added that this hypothesis proposes only a probability, not a scientific certainty. However, the doc-

---

[2] Pius XII, "Humani Generis," no. 36, August 12, 1950, Vatican, http://w2.vatican.va/content/pius-xii/en/encyclicals/documents/hf_p-xii_enc_12081950_humani-generis.html, (accessed June 2, 2015).

trine of faith invariably affirms that man's spiritual soul is created directly by God. According to the hypothesis mentioned, it is possible that the human body, following the order impressed by the Creator on the energies of life, could have been gradually prepared in the forms of antecedent living beings. However, the human soul, on which man's humanity definitively depends, cannot emerge from matter, since the soul is of a spiritual nature.[3]

Due to this infusion of a rational soul, human beings are different in kind from the lower animals, who have only sensitive souls incapable of reason. As *homo sapiens*, that is wise men, we are called to an end that we cannot attain by our own efforts. In order to attain our final end in heaven, experienced by the beatific vision, we need the help of divine grace. This final cause profoundly distinguishes us from non-rational animals whose sensitive souls die with their bodies.

Pre-historic Eras

Pre-history refers to the period of time prior to written records. (Note well that the absence of written historical records does not mean that all pre-historical ages are prior to the invention of writing.) This time is

---

[3] John Paul II, "Humans are Spiritual and Corporeal Beings," April 16, 1986, Interdisciplinary Dictionary of Religion and Science, inters.org/printpdf/John-Paul-II-Catechesis-Spiritual-Corporeal, (accessed June 2, 2016).

typically broken up into three periods: Stone Age, Bronze Age, and Iron Age. The Stone Age is divided into the Old Stone Age, and the New Stone age. During the last two ages, the Bronze and Iron Ages, writing was invented and developed. The dates used for all of these eras are approximate.

Old Stone Age/Paleolithic Age by Viktor Vasnetsov (1882-1885)⁴

During the Old Stone Age (c. 2.5 million years – 8,000 BC) human beings, or in accordance with Evolutionary theory, early hominids, were nomadic. They obtained their food by hunting and gathering hence the name nomadic hunter-gatherers. In their struggle for survival these nomads used fire, clothing, and tools. Around one million years ago, the West

---

⁴ http://www.picture.art-catalog.ru/picture.php?id_picture=3316, "Imaginative depiction of the Stone Age, by Viktor Vasnetsov," photograph, http://commons.wikimedia.org/wiki/File%3A%D0%9A%D0%B0%D0%BC%D0%B5%D0%BD%D0%BD%D1%8B%D0%B9_%D0%B2%D0%B5%D0%BA_(1).jpg, (accessed June 4, 2015).

Asian and African nomads, through a series of migrations, reached East Asia.[5]

New Stone Age/Neolithic Age

In the Neolithic Age (c. 8,000 – 3,000 BC), some people settled down and began to farm, raise animals, and grow grain. Weapons for warfare were also made and used during this period. During the last phase of the Neolithic Age, copper was used for tools. The Copper Age, or Calcolithic age, was replaced by the Bronze Age.[6]

Bronze Age

The main distinctive feature of the Bronze Age (c. 3,000-1000 BC) was smelting of both copper and tin in order to combine the two metals to create bronze, a metal that is harder than copper. During this age, writing was invented. Some of the earliest evidence of Asian writing are the oracle bones upon which are inscribed the most ancient known Chinese characters.[7]

---

[5] Patricia Ebrey, Anne Walthall, and James Palais, *East Asia: A Cultural, Social, and Political History* (Belmont: Wadsworth, 2009), 2.

[6] Craig G. Benjamin, *Foundations of Eastern Civilization*, Lectures 1-24 (Chantilly: The Great Courses, 2013), 41.

[7] Ebrey, Walthall, and Palais, 12.

Eastern Civilization from a Catholic Viewpoint

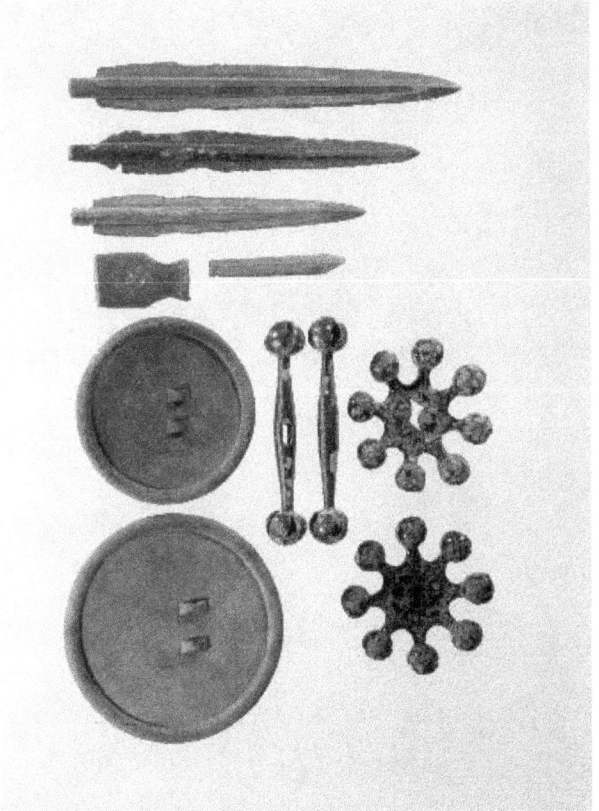

Bronze Age Artifacts, Daegok-ri, Hwasun, Korea[8]

---

[8] 국립중앙박물관(National Museum of Korea), "Bronze Artifacts from Daegok-ri, Hwasun, National Treasure of South Korea No. 143," photograph, http://www.commons.wikimedia.org/wiki/File%3A%ED%99%94%EC%88%9C_%EB%8C%80%EA%B3%A1%EB%A6%AC_%EC%B2%AD%EB%8F%99%EA%B8%B0_%EC%9D%BC%EA%B4%84.jpg, (accessed June 4, 2015).

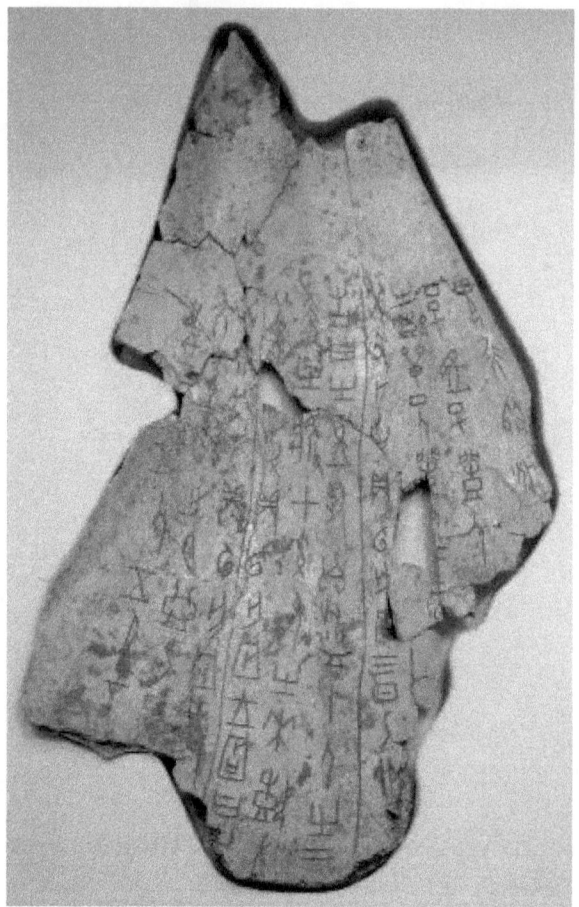

Oracle Bone[9]

Iron Age

During the Iron Age (c. 300s BC), iron was smelted and then shaped into tools or weapons. Agricultural techniques continued to advance in this

---

[9] BabelStone, "Oracle bone from the reign of King Wu Ding (late Shang dynasty)," photograph, http://www.commons.wikimedia.org/wiki/File%3AShang_dynasty_inscribed_scapula.jpg, (accessed June 7, 2015).

age.[10]

The Chinese Bronze Age Master Sword Maker
Ou Lezi[11]

Civilization: Strengths and Weaknesses

There are a variety of explanations for the births, declines and renewals of the various civilizations that make up Eastern Civilization. We will look at three ancient Eastern explanations represented by Confucius, Laozi, and Han Feizi. These three men are considered founders of Confucianism, Daoism, and Legalism which we will study in subsequent chapters.

---

[10] Grant Hardy, *Great Minds of the Eastern Intellectual Tradition*, Lectures 19-36 (Chantilly: The Great Courses, 2011), 160-161.
[11] Unknown Photographer, "Ou Yezi making sword painting in Ou Yezi temple of Longquan City," photograph, http://commons.wikimedia.org/wiki/File%3AOu_Yezi_m ake_sword.jpg, (accessed June 4, 2015).

The Chinese philosopher Confucius (551-479 BC) held that a strong civilization depends on people living out their designated hierarchical role in society by the observance of virtue especially the following: benevolence, filial piety, integrity, loyalty, honest, reverence/respect, and ritual decorum.[12]

Laozi (Lao Tzu) (500 BC) is credited with writing the *Tao Te Ching*. (This is not certain since there is little evidence that Laozi existed.) The *Tao Te Ching* rejected the idea that active pursuit of virtue, especially by political leaders, strengthens civilization. Rather, according to this document, if human beings are allowed and encouraged to follow their inner goodness by uniting themselves with the natural order called the Way (Dao), the result will be harmony among people and with nature.[13] In accordance with a particular concept of the feminine nature, rulers, consequently, should be more passive than active. Reflecting this belief, the *Tao Te Ching* states:

~ Tao Te Ching Verse 32 ~

Tao is eternal, one without a second
simple indeed
yet so subtle that no one can master it
If princes and kings could just hold it
All things would flock to their kingdom
Heaven and Earth would rejoice
And with the dripping of sweet dew

---

[12] Ebrey, Walthall, and Palais, 26.
[13] Ebrey, Walthall, and Palais, 29-30.

Everyone would live in harmony,
not by official decree,
but by their own inner goodness.[14]

~ *Tao Te Ching* Verse 57 ~

1. A state may be ruled by (measures of) correction; weapons of war may be used with crafty dexterity; (but) the kingdom is made one's own (only) by freedom from action and purpose.

2. How do I know that it is so? By these facts:—In the kingdom the multiplication of prohibitive enactments increases the poverty of the people; the more implements to add to their profit that the people have, the greater disorder is there in the state and clan; the more acts of crafty dexterity that men possess, the more do strange contrivances appear; the more display there is of legislation, the more thieves and robbers there are.

3. Therefore a sage has said, 'I will do nothing (of purpose), and the people will be transformed of themselves; I will be fond of keeping still, and the people will of themselves become correct. I will take no trouble about it, and the people will of themselves become rich; I will

---

[14] Lao Tzu, *Tao Te Ching*, trans. Jonathan Star (New York: Penguin Group, 2001), 42.

manifest no ambition, and the people will of themselves attain to the primitive simplicity.'[15]

~ *Tao Te Ching* Verse 61 ~

1. What makes a great state is its being (like) a low-lying, down-flowing (stream);—it becomes the center to which tend (all the small states) under heaven.

2. (To illustrate from) the case of all females:—the female always overcomes the male by her stillness. Stillness may be considered (a sort of) abasement.

3. Thus it is that a great state, by condescending to small states, gains them for itself; and that small states, by abasing themselves to a great state, win it over to them. In the one case the abasement leads to gaining adherents, in the other case to procuring favor.

4. The great state only wishes to unite men together and nourish them; a small state only wishes to be received by, and to serve, the other. Each gets what it desires, but the great

---

[15] "The Tao Teh King, or The Tao and Its Characteristics by Lao-Tse." trans. James Legge, Project Gutenberg, http://www.gutenberg.org/files/216/216-h/216-h.htm#link2H_PART (accessed June 7, 2015).

state must learn to abase itself.[16]

Han Feizi (c. 280-233 BC) was an ancient Chinese philosopher identified with the school known as Legalism. According to Legalism the strength of a civilization depends not on the virtue of its members, nor on a live and let live attitude of leaders, but rather on the enforcement of uniform laws by a strong leader. What is essential to Legalism is that the leader centralizes power in himself and enforces laws vigorously. Whether he is virtuous or values passivity is of less importance.[17]

~ Han Feizi on Law ~

The Law no more makes exceptions for men of high station than the plumb line bends to accommodate a crooked place in the wood. What the law has decreed the wise man cannot dispute nor the brave man venture to contest. When faults are to be punished, the highest minister cannot escape; when good is to be rewarded, the lowest peasant must not be passed over. Hence, for correcting the faults of superiors, chastising the misdeeds of subordinates, restoring order, exposing error, checking excess, remedying evil, and unifying the standards of the people, nothing can compare to law. For putting fear into officials, awing the people, wiping out wantonness and

---

[16] "The Tao Teh King, or The Tao and Its Characteristics by Lao-Tse."

[17] Ebrey, Walthall, and Palais, 31.

sloth, and preventing lies and deception nothing can compare to penalties. If penalties are heavy, men dare not use high position to abuse the humble; if laws are clearly defined, superiors will be honored and their rights will not be invaded. If they are honored and their rights are inviolable, then the ruler will be strong and will hold fast to what is essential. Hence the former kings held laws in high esteem and handed them down to posterity.[18]

The Catholic understanding of what makes a civilization strong and lasts includes the observance of law, the practice of virtue, the ability to contemplate, and reliance on a reality that transcends this world called grace. Catholicism agrees with Confucius and Lao Tzu that human nature is essentially good but also shares, along with Han Feizi, a distrust of human nature's ability to be good. For Catholics, this distrust does not stem from a belief that men are innately self-centered and amoral but rather stems from an acknowledgement of original and personal sin. In order for an individual and civilizations to develop properly, therefore, humans need to cooperate with grace that builds upon, augments and transforms their good natures, which are wounded but not destroyed by sin. This grace, which ultimately comes through Christ, is received in prayer and actualized by virtue.

---

[18] Han Fei Tzu, *Han Fei: Tzu Basic Writings*, trans. Burton Watson (New York: Columbia University Press, 1964), 28-29.

Quiz 1 for Chapter 1

1. Define the word civilization etymologically.

2-3. Explain in at least two way with reference to one papal document/talk how man is not simply a highly developed animal.

2.

3.

4. State the official Catholic teaching on evolution. Include in your answer the soul, and consciousness.

4. With reference to writing, define the prehistorical age.

5-7. List the three prehistorical ages and then provide a significant advance for each age.

5.

6.

7.

8-9. What are the oracle bones and from what period of time do they come from?

8.

9.

10-13. With respect to the essential elements of a healthy and lasting civilization distinguish the following from one another: Confucianism, Daoism, Legalism and Catholicism.

10.

11.

12.

13.

Chapter 2: Ancient China and India

Introduction

In this chapter, we will study East Asian civilizations by examining the early history of China and India. While looking at China, we will be introduced to the Shang Dynasty, China's earliest recorded civilization. Then, we will look at the Zhou dynasty. This section on China will conclude with an overview of the *Yijing* (I Ching), known in English as the *Book of Changes*.

In the following section, two key texts from ancient India will be surveyed: the Vedas and the Upanishads (also spelled *Upaniṣads*). Finally, we will close this chapter with Indian philosopher Uddalaka who lived during the 800s BC.

The Shang Dynasty

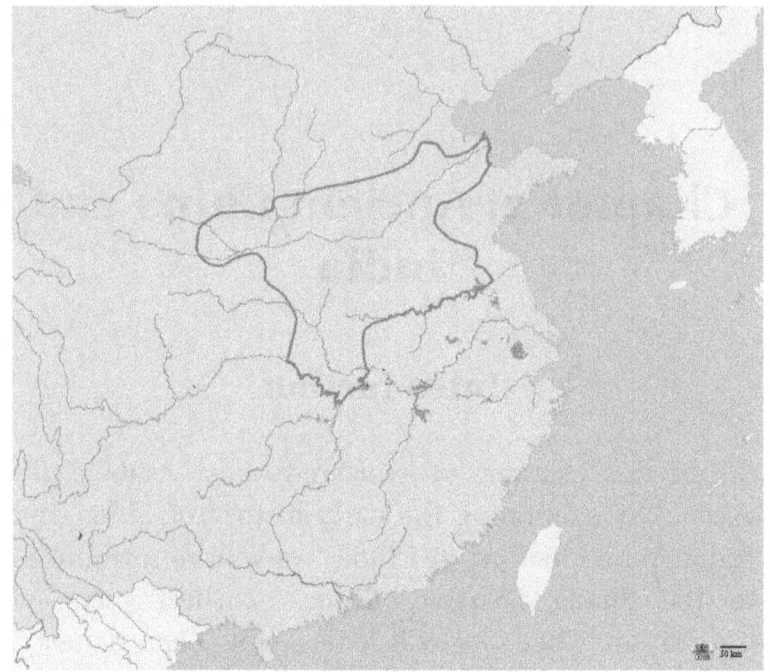

Location of the Shang Dynasty[19]

Some historians maintain that the Shang dynasty (c. 1600-1045 BC) was not the first Chinese dynasty. Despite convincing archaeological and literary evidence, these scholars propose that China's first dynasty, a period of time when a powerful family reigns over a kingdom, was the Xia dynasty (c. 2070-1600 BC).[20]

---

[19] Lamassu Design, "Location of the Shang Dynasty," map, http://commons.wikimedia.org/wiki/File%3AShang_dynasty.svg, (accessed June 9, 2015)

[20] Craig G. Benjamin, *Foundations of Eastern Civilization*, Lectures 1-24 (Chantilly: The Great Courses,

Around 1600 BC, the Shang Dynasty rose to power. Concrete evidence of this dynasty is found in the oracle bones mentioned in the previous chapter. When these bones were discovered in the 1800s, they were mistaken for magical dragon bones and ground up for "medicines". Eventually scholars found out about these bones and started translating the ancient characters etched into them. Their translations provided significant information about the Shang dynasty.

Much warfare occurred during the Shang Dynasty. As a result, military weapons and tactics developed. One example is the Shang use of horse-drawn chariots around 1200 BC. The Shang Dynasty not only defended their centrally unified dynasty with military might, but also strove to bring about unity through ritual practices. Two principle practices they sanctioned were fortune telling and ancestor worship. Shang kings participated directly in these two rituals as priests who, they claimed, were capable of communicating with the dead.[21] The main god of this time that the Shang kings worshipped was named Shangdi meaning "Lord on High." According to myth, Shangdi lived in a heavenly city called Shang along with Shang ancestors. Sacrifices, including human

---

2013), 44-46. Sometimes students learn the major dynasties of China by singing them according to the "Frere Jacques" tune. Shang, Zhou, Qin, Han, Shang, Zhou, Qin, Han, Sui, Tang, Song, Sui, Tang, Song, Yuan, Ming, Qing, Republic, Yuan, Ming, Qing, Republic, Mao Ze Dong, Mao Ze Dong. See http://ksuweb.kennesaw.edu/~mracel/Documents/ogt/Chinese%20Dynasty%20Song.pdf

[21] Benjamin, 58-63.

sacrifices, were offered up to Shangdi and other lesser gods.[22]

17th century Jesuit missionaries, in an attempt of inculturation, proposed to the Chinese that Shangdi, in his true essence, is the God of Christianity. The Chinese worship of Shangdi, further claimed the Jesuits, had over time become distorted. Both Dominicans and Franciscans protested the Jesuit's attempted Christian use of the name Shangdi and the Jesuit's tolerance of Chinese Catholics honoring their dead.[23] In 1645, Pope Innocent X decreed that the "Chinese rites," promoted by the Jesuits, were not to be used.[24] Below, is an excerpt from *The True Meaning of the Lord of Heaven* by the Jesuit priest and Servant of God Matteo Ricci whose beatification is currently being considered by Rome.

~ The True Meaning of the Lord of Heaven ~

103. He who is called the Lord of Heaven in my humble country is He who is called Shang-ti (Sovereign on High) [Lord On High or Shangdi] in Chinese. He is not, however, the same as the carved image of the Taoist Jade Emperor who is

---

[22] Alvyn Austin, *China's Millions* (Grand Rapids: Wm. B. Eerdmans, 2007), 155-156.

[23] Austin, 156.

[24] Michela Fontana, *Matteo Ricci: A Jesuit in the Ming Court* (Lanham: Rowman & Littlefield Publishers, 2011), 291-294; "Father Matteo Ricci's Beatification Cause Reopened", Agenzia Fides, http://www.fides.org/en/news/25874?idnews=25874&lan=eng#.VF5r_-ktC1s, (accessed November 8, 2014)

described as the Supreme Lord of the Black Pavilions of Heaven, for he was no more than a recluse on Wu-tang mountain. Since he was a man, how could he have been the Sovereign of heaven and earth?[25]

Below is an image of modern day, Chinese, ancestor veneration.

Chinese Daoist Ancestor Worship[26]

Modern forms of Fortune telling, traceable to the Shang dynasty, include palm reading, face reading, shaking bamboo sticks (*Kau Cim*), astrology, use of

---

[25] Matteo Ricci, "The True Meaning of the Lord of Heaven," Christendom Awake, http://www.christendom-awake.org/pages/dlancash/chineseworks/tmlh.html, (accessed November 8, 2014).

[26] Lai Chuen Siu, "A Taoist rite for ancestor worship at the Xiao ancestral temple of Chaoyang, Shantou, Guangdong," photograph, http://commons.wikimedia.org/wiki/File%3ATaoist_ceremony_at_Xiao_ancestral_templ e_in_Chaoyang%2C_Shantou%2C_Guangdong_(inside)_ (4).jpg, (accessed June 9, 2015).

grass stalks and coins, numerology, and use of revered books.[27]

Kau Cim in Hong Kong[28]

The Zhou Dynasty

The Western Zhou dynasty (c. 1045-770 BC) replaced the Shang dynasty after the last Shang King

---

[27] Ching-Huang Wu, *Fortune-Telling: A Science of Mystery* (Xlibris, 2011), 5-10.

[28] Ted Chan in Hong Kong, February 2007, "The act of "Kau Cim" at Wong Tai Sin," photograph, http://en.wikipedia.org/wiki/File:Kaucim.jpg, (accessed June 9, 2015). "I, the copyright holder of this work, hereby grant the permission to copy, distribute and/or modify this document under the terms of the GNU Free Documentation License, Version 1.2 or any later version published by the Free Software Foundation; with no Invariant Sections, no Front-Cover Texts, and no Back-Cover Texts."

was defeated by the Zhou King Wu in the Battle of Muye (c. 1045 BC).[29] It is called "Western" since its rulers lived in the Western portion of China.[30] When replacing the Shang dynasty, the Zhou promoted themselves as morally superior to the supposedly immoral rule of the Shang. Out of this narrative developed a theory of kings that is similar to the Western idea of the Divine Right of Kings. The Eastern version is called the Mandate of Heaven. According to the Mandate of Heaven, as explained in poetry from the Zhou period contained in the *Book of Odes*, the gods in heaven punished the corrupt Shang by allowing the upright Zhou to defeat them in battle and replace their rule. The belief that rulers are to live upright lives and if not the gods will punish them influenced Chinese politics through all its dynasties until the final Qing dynasty (1644-1912). The Mandate of Heaven was repeatedly appealed to in order to explain the fall of one dynasty and the legitimacy of its successor.[31]

Due to a feud between the Western Zhou King You and a powerful Eastern ruler, who was the father of King You's wife, the Western Zhou dynasty fell in 770 BC. King You had enraged the Eastern ruler by dismissing his daughter, to whom he was married, and replacing her with a concubine. In the beginning of the Eastern Zhou dynasty, the capital shifted

---

[29] Benjamin, 99; Ebrey, Walthall, and Palais, 16.
[30] Benjamin, 100.
[31] Benjamin, 91-92; Alfred J. Andrea, James H. Overfield, *The Human Record: Sources of Global History*, Volume I to 1700 (Boston: Houghton Mifflin, 2001), 27.

eastward, hence the name Eastern Zhou dynasty (770-256 BC). This dynasty was divided into The Spring and Autumn Period (722-481 BC) and the Warring States Period (480-256 BC). During these two periods the Zhou Kingdom fragmented into many warring states. Much bloodshed occurred during these frequent wars. Gradually, one warring kingdom, the Qin State, emerged as the dominant power and in 256 BC overthrew the last Zhou king.[32]

Yijing (I Ching)

The *Yijing*, known in English as the *Book of Changes*, was written around 680 BC during the Eastern Zhou Dynasty. This book detailed a divination system consisting of lines, some of which are broken, that increasingly replaced the use of oracle bones.[33] Under the great philosopher Confucius (551-479), the *Yijing* was chosen to be one of five foundational books called the Five Classics consisting of the *Yijing*, the collection of poetry to the gods and ancestors called the *Book of Odes*, the *Book of Documents* of Zhou rulers and officials, the *Book of Rites*, and a book that chronicles history has named the *Spring and Autumn Annals*.[34] Below are the 64 hexagrams from the *Yijing* that were and are used in divination.

---

[32] Benjamin, 92-98.
[33] Benjamin, 94, 102.
[34] Benjamin, 102; Ebrey, Walthall, and Palais, 46.

Eastern Civilization from a Catholic Viewpoint

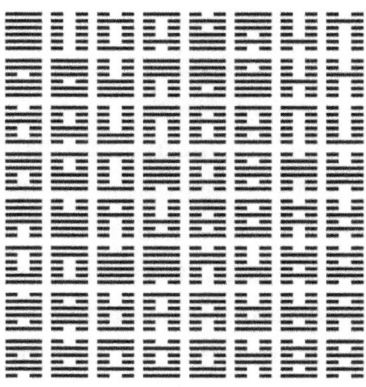

64 Hexagrams of the *Yijing*[35]

Vedas

We will now shift our attention away from China to another very ancient Eastern Civilization, India. As with China, India has a set of foundational writings that greatly shaped its civilization. One such work is the *Vedas*, written in Sanskrit, a language that is related to the European languages.[36] This collection is of the oldest writings from India. It consists of theology, philosophy, laws, religious rituals, and poetry. For the Hindus, the four books of the *Vedas* are their most sacred texts.

---

[35] enoc, "Los 64 hexagramas I Ching," diagram, http://commons.wikimedia.org/wiki/File%3AKing_Wen_(I_Ching).svg, (accessed June 11, 2015).

[36] Benjamin, 22. This is because the early speakers of Sanskrit were Indo-European, called the Aryans, who originated from regions now associated with southern Russian and the Ukraine. As Romance languages stem from Latin, non-Romance European languages stem from the Indo-European language family which includes Sanskrit, Russian, Greek and, in part, English.

A central re-occurring theme in the Vedas that is key to understanding much of Indian thought is the caste system. A caste system hierarchically orders people. For example, in many Western countries how much money a person has or earns defines his social status. In contrast, the Indian caste system was understood as hereditary according to which people are born into a certain social class whose rights differ from classes above or below it.[37] The Indian hierarchy is defined not by wealth but by purity, understood spiritually as reflected in and through the physical world. In accordance with caste system purity rules, strictly observant Hindus do not marry nor eat with anyone outside of their caste.[38]

According to the Rig Veda, the caste system first began when the first man killed himself. Out of his body, various human groups were formed. The Brahmans, the highest class, were formed from his head, the Kshatrias from his hands, the Vaishias from his thighs, and the Sudras from his feet.[39]

---

[37] Benjamin, 22-24; Subhamoy Das and Manoj Sadasivan, "What are the Vedas? A Brief Introduction," about religion, http://hinduism.about.com/cs/vedasvedanta/a/aa120103a.htm, (accessed June 11, 2015).

[38] Mark. W. Muesse, *Great World Religions: Hinduism* (Chantilly: Great Courses, 2003), 19. R.K. Pruthi, *Indian Caste System* (New Delhi: Discovery Publishing House, 2004), 5.

[39] R.K. Pruthi, *Indian Caste System* (New Delhi: Discovery Publishing House, 2004), 1.

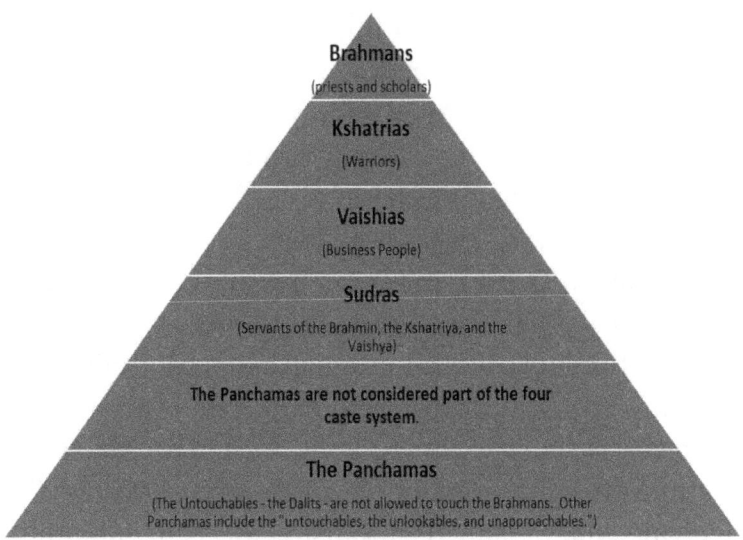

The Caste System[40]

Upanishads (Upaniṣads)

The Upanishads (c. 900 – 500 BC) are the parts of the Vedas that deal specifically with philosophy, spirituality, and prayer. Key topics they discuss include, according to their Sanskrit names, samsara, karma, dharma, moksha, Atman and Brahman. In Sanskrit, samsara means "a gliding through." It is used in reference to souls that, according to Brahmanism and Hinduism, are reincarnated in different life forms. Karma means fate and deeds. In the Upanishads, it means justice that is cosmically determined by bad deeds and good deeds. Dharma translates into English as correct, or right, in the sense of right

---

[40] The information for the diagram comes from R.K. Pruthi, *Indian Caste System* (New Delhi: Discovery Publishing House, 2004), 6, 2-4.

action. Moksha refers to liberation from the cycle of reincarnation. Atman in English signifies the soul or the essence of the individual while Brahman signifies the universal soul or ultimate reality that permeates and sustains all that exists.[41]

The following excerpt is central teaching of the Upanishads. In this passage, the individual soul is identified with the Brahman. This means that whatever distinctions we think exist between individuals and that which sustains all in existence is an illusion. Even the various Brahman gods are but an illusion of the one Brahman reality of which all are part.[42] The doctrine taught here is monism. Monism maintains that ultimately no distinction between individuals exists since all is fundamentally one reality. The key to be freed from the recurring cycles of samsara, where individuals transmigrate from one life form to another, is to let go of desire. When this occurs, the individual then realizes that all is one and becomes "merged in Brahman."[43]

According to Catholicism, even when experiencing the highest stages of mysticism, we do not lose our identity as we draw closer to God. Instead, we become more ourselves in accordance with our true identity that, even though related, always remains distinct from others and from our Creator. Our relationship

---

[41] Hardy, 18; Online Etymology Dictionary, http://etymonline.com/, (accessed June 12, 2015).

[42] Hardy, 30.

[43] *The Brhadaranyaka Upaniṣad*, trans. Swami Madhavananda (Almora: Advaita Ashrama, 1950), 4.4.6, p. 717.

with God, consequently, is never absent from desire as Benedict XVI states in his encyclical *Deus Caritas Est* (*God is Love*). Here, the Holy Father, defines desirous love (*eros*) as ascending, possessive love from human beings to God and descending love as that which comes down to us from God. These loves, Benedict XVI writes, "can never be completely separated."[44] In explaining this he writes:

~ Benedict XVI's *God is Love* ~

The more the two, in their different aspects, find a proper unity in the one reality of love, the more the true nature of love in general is realized. Even if *eros* is at first mainly covetous and ascending, a fascination for the great promise of happiness, in drawing near to the other, it is less and less concerned with itself, increasingly seeks the happiness of the other, is concerned more and more with the beloved, bestows itself and wants to "be there for" the other. The element of *agape* thus enters into this love, for otherwise *eros* is impoverished and even loses its own nature. On the other hand, man cannot live by oblative, descending love alone. He cannot always give, he must also receive. Anyone who wishes to give love must also receive love as a gift. Certainly, as the

---

[44] Benedict XVI, "Deus Caritas Est," December 25, 2005, no. 7, The Vatican, http://w2.vatican.va/content/benedict-xvi/en/encyclicals/documents/hf_ben-xvi_enc_20051225_deus-caritas-est.html (accessed June 122, 2015).

Lord tells us, one can become a source from which rivers of living water flow (cf. Jn 7:37-38). Yet to become such a source, one must constantly drink anew from the original source, which is Jesus Christ, from whose pierced heart flows the love of God (cf. Jn 19:34).

In the account of Jacob's ladder, the Fathers of the Church saw this inseparable connection between ascending and descending love, between *eros* which seeks God and *agape* which passes on the gift received, symbolized in various ways. In that biblical passage we read how the Patriarch Jacob saw in a dream, above the stone which was his pillow, a ladder reaching up to heaven, on which the angels of God were ascending and descending (cf. Gen 28:12; Jn 1:51). A particularly striking interpretation of this vision is presented by Pope Gregory the Great in his *Pastoral Rule*. He tells us that the good pastor must be rooted in contemplation. Only in this way will he be able to take upon himself the needs of others and make them his own: *"per pietatis viscera in se infirmitatem caeterorum transferat"*. Saint Gregory speaks in this context of Saint Paul, who was borne aloft to the most exalted mysteries of God, and hence, having descended once more, he was able to become all things to all men (cf. 2 Cor 12:2-4; 1 Cor 9:22). He also points to the example of Moses, who entered the tabernacle time and again, remaining in dialogue with God, so that when he emerged he could be at the service of his people.

"Within [the tent] he is borne aloft through contemplation, while without he is completely engaged in helping those who suffer: *intus in contemplationem rapitur, foris infirmantium negotiis urgetur.*"[45]

Compare and contrast Benedict XVI's Catholic explanation of self, God, love and desire with the following excerpt from the Upanishads.

~ Atman = Brahman ~

From the *The Brhadaranyaka Upanishad*

That self [Atman] is indeed Brahman, as well as identified with the intellect, the Manas and the vital force, with the eyes and ears, with earth, water, air and the ether, with fire, and what is other than fire, with desire and the absence of desire, with anger and the absence of anger, with righteousness and unrighteousness, with everything-identified, as is well known, with this (what is perceived) and with that (what is inferred). As it does and acts, so it becomes...That self which thus transmigrates [reincarnates] is indeed Brahman, the Supreme Self that is beyond ....Being identified with righteousness and unrighteousness it becomes identified with everything. Everything is the effect of righteousness and unrighteousness:

---

[45] Benedict XVI, "Deus Caritas Est," December 25, 2005, no. 7.

whatever is differentiated is the result of these two. The self, on attaining it, becomes identified with that. In short, *identified, as is well known*, i.e. with objects that are perceived, *and* therefore *with that*.... Upanishad says, "He, who longs for objects of desire, making much of the, is born along with those desires in places where he will realize them" (III, ii. 2). Therefore the self is identified with desire alone....Thus does the man who desires (transmigrates). But the man who does not desire (never transmigrates). Of him who is without desires, who is free from desires, the objects of whose desire have been attained, and to whom all objects of desire are but the Self-the organs do not depart. Being but Brahman, he is merged in Brahman.[46]

Uddalaka

Uddalaka (c. 800s BC) was a famous Upanishad sage. In the account of a Banyan fruit, he vividly represents Monistic doctrine. His teaching that individual identity is an illusion is contained in this short story from the Chandogya Upanishad.

~ The Self as Nothing ~

1. "Bring me a fruit of that nyagrodha (banyan) tree." "Here it is' venerable Sir." "Break it." "It is

---

[46] *The Brhadaranyaka Upaniṣad*, trans. Swami Madhavananda (Almora: Advaita Ashrama, 1950), 4.4.5-4.4.6, pp. 712- 717.

broken, venerable Sir." "What do you see there?" "These seeds, exceedingly small, "Break one of these, my son." "It is broken, venerable Sir." "What do you see there?" "Nothing at all, venerable Sir."

2. The father said: "That subtle essence, my dear, which you do not perceive there—from that very essence this great nyagrodha arises. Believe me, my dear.

3. "Now, that which is the subtle essence—in it all that exists has its self. That is the True. That is the Self. That thou art, Svetaketu." "Please, venerable Sir, give me further instruction," said the son. "So be it, my dear," the father replied.[47]

Quiz 2 for Chapter 2

1-2. The Shang dynasty (c. 1600-1045 BC) established two principle practices that became foundational to Eastern civilization. Name these two practices.

1.

2.

3-4. Name and explain the political theory of kings that came about after the Western Zhou dynasty (c.

---

[47] "Chandogya Upanishad," part 6, chap. 12, 1-3, trans., Swami Nikhilananda, SwamiJ.com http://www.swamij.com/upanishad-chandogya.htm (accessed June 12, 2015).

1045-771 BC) replaced the Shang dynasty.

3.

4.

5. The *Yijing* (*I Ching* or Book of Changes) was written during the Eastern Zhou dynasty. Choose from the following list what it is mainly about.

a. laws

b. ritual

c. divination

d. ancestor worship

6-7. Where were the *Vedas* written and how, according to the *Vedas*, ought the social system it is referring to be organized?

6.

7.

8-13. Place the following terms across from their definitions: karma, Brahman, moksha, samsara, dharma, and Atman.

8.	Reincarnation
9.	Cosmic justice
10.	Right Action
11.	Liberation
12.	Individual Soul
13.	Universal Soul or Reality

14-17. Compare and contrast Benedict XVI's Catholic explanation of self, God, love and desire with these realities as presented by *The Brhadaranyaka Upaniṣad* and by Uddalaka in the *Chandogya Upanishad*.

Chapter 3: Vedanta Hinduism

Introduction

As mentioned in the previous chapter, Hindus believe the *Vedas* to be sacred text. Hindus consider six Hindu philosophical schools to be orthodox, all of which revere the *Vedas*. (Veda means knowledge in Sanskrit.)[48] One school, the Vedanta, is named after a part of the *Vedas* called the Vedanta, meaning knowledge (*veda*) and end (*anta*) since it comes at the end of the *Vedas*.[49] Since the 700s, this school has been the most dominant of the six: Vedanta, Yoga, Samkhya, Nyaya, Vaisheshika, and Mimamsa. In this chapter, the Vedanta will be studied with reference to the three of its most influential philosophers. Then, in the following chapter the Hindu school of Yoga, which is well-known in the West, will be examined.

Before doing so, the term Hinduism needs to be

---

[48] Jeanneane D. Fowler, *Perspectives of Reality: An Introduction to the Philosophy of Hinduism* (Brighton: Sussex Academic Press, 2002), ix.

[49] Fowler, 46; Grant Hardy, *Great Minds of the Eastern Intellectual Tradition*, Lectures 19-36 (Chantilly: The Teaching Company, 2011), 24.

briefly discussed. The term "Hindu" is of Persian origin and means Indians or people from "the region of the Indus."[50] Consequently, the idea of a religion called Hinduism is not a term that arose in land associated with India. If misapplied, it can lead the user to assume Hinduism refers to a religion of India that is united by similar beliefs and practices. In reality "Hinduism" is characterized by diversity in both beliefs and practices as will be evident.[51]

Shankara and Vedanta Absolute Monism or non-Dualism

Shankara (aka Śaṅkara, 788-822 AD) wrote on the spiritual and philosophical sections of the Vedas called the Upanishads, another name for the Vedanta. As explained by Fowler, Shankara identified four statements from the Upanishads as the basis of his philosophy. These four are:

1. Brahman is Consciousness
2. I am Brahman
3. That you are
4. This Atman is Brahman[52]

In order to understand why for Shankara these

---

[50] "Hindu," Online Etymology Dictionary, http://etymonline.com/index.php?term=Hindu&allowed_in_frame=0, (accessed July 10, 2015).

[51] Mark W. Muesse, *Great World Religions: Hinduism*, Course Guidebook (Chantilly: The Great Courses, 2003), 3.

[52] Fowler, 239.

statements underlie his absolute monism or an unqualified non-Dualism, the terms Brahman and Atman need to be defined. Brahman, as defined by the *Oxford Dictionary of Hinduism* is "the power underlying and connecting all things, i.e. the universe in its entirety."[53] Atman, on the other hand, refers to the self in a reflexive manner or an individual, living body.[54] In other words, Brahman is the universal, divine energy that relates all individual things to each other. Atman are the individual things. According to Shankara, it only appears that these individual things exist. In reality, all that exists without any qualification is Brahman, for Atman is Brahman which is, claims Shankara, what we all are.

Ramanuja and Vedanta Qualified non-Dualism

Ramanuja (c. 1017-1137 AD) also interpreted the *Vedas* in a non-Dualistic manner. However, he rejected Shankara's belief that even qualities are but an illusion. For Ramanuja, differences of the world are not merely an illusion. Instead, he argued for the existence of plurality as qualities of the Brahman. Understood in this manner, the entire cosmos is the body of Brahman and its parts. The various parts of Brahman although not distinct from Brahman are,

---

[53] W. J. Johnson, *Oxford Dictionary of Hinduism* (New York: Oxford University Press, 2009), 64.
[54] Johnson, 37.

nonetheless, qualitatively different:55

~ From Ramanuja's Commentary on the *Vedanta Sutras* ~

We now turn to the numerous texts which, according to the view of our opponent, negative [negate] the existence of plurality.—'Where there is duality as it were' (Bri. Up. IV, 5, 15); 'There is not any plurality here; from death to death goes he who sees here any plurality' (Bri. Up. IV, 4, 19); 'But when for him the Self alone has become all, by what means, and whom, should he see?' (Bri. Up. IV, 5, 15) &c.—But what all these texts deny is only plurality in so far as contradicting that unity of the world which depends on its being in its entirety an effect of Brahman, and having Brahman for its inward ruling principle and its true Self. They do not, on the other hand, deny that plurality on Brahman's part which depends on its intention to become manifold—a plurality proved by the text 'May I be many, may I grow forth' (Ch. Up. VI, 2, 3). Nor can our opponent urge against this that, owing to the denial of plurality contained in other passages this last text refers to something not real; for it is an altogether laughable assertion that Scripture should at first teach the doctrine, difficult to comprehend, that plurality as suggested by Perception and the other means of Knowledge

---

55 Grant Hardy, *Great Minds of the Eastern Intellectual Tradition*, Lectures 19-36 (Chantilly: The Teaching Company, 2011), 29.

belongs to Brahman also, and should afterwards negative [negate] this very doctrine![56]

In attempting to uphold both plurality and a monistic view of the world he further argued the following:

> Next as to the assertion that all difference presented in our cognition—as of jars, pieces of cloth and the like—is unreal because such difference does not persist. This view, we maintain, is altogether erroneous, springs in fact from the neglect of distinguishing between persistence and non-persistence on the one hand, and the relation between what sublates and what is sublated on the other hand. Where two cognitions are mutually contradictory, there the latter relation holds good, and there is non-persistence of what is sublated. But jars, pieces of cloth and the like, do not contradict one another, since they are separate in place and time. If on the other hand the non-existence of a thing is cognized at the same time and the same place where and when its existence is cognized, we have a mutual contradiction of two cognitions, and then the stronger one sublates the other cognition which thus comes to an end. But when of a thing that is perceived in connection

---

[56] Ramanuja, *The Vedanta-Sutras with the Commentary by Ramanuja Sacred Books of the East*, Volume 48, trans. George Thibaut, (1904) The Great Siddhanta, Project Gutenberg, http://www.gutenberg.org/cache/epub/7297/pg7297.html, (accessed June 29, 2015).

with some place and time, the non-existence is perceived in connection with some other place and time, there arises no contradiction; how then should the one cognition sublate the other? or how can it be said that of a thing absent at one time and place there is absence at other times and places also? In the case of the snake-rope, there arises a cognition of non-existence in connection with the given place and time; hence there is contradiction, one judgment sublates the other and the sublated cognition comes to an end. But the circumstance of something which is seen at one time and in one place not persisting at another time and in another place is not observed to be invariably accompanied by falsehood, and hence mere non-persistence of this kind does not constitute a reason for unreality. To say, on the other hand, that what is real because it persists, is to prove what is proved already, and requires no further proof.[57]

Madhva and Vedanta Dualism

Madhva (c. 1199-1278 AD) rejected both Shankara's and Ramanuja's belief that difference is an illusion and we all are one. In the case of Shankara, monism is understood in an absolute sense. For Shankara, even qualities are but an illusion. While accepting that qualitative differences do actually exist, Ramanuja still held to a pantheistic understanding of reality since he saw these differences are but aspects

---

[57] Ramanuja, Volume 48.

of God. Madhva, rejected the pantheism that does not acknowledge distinction between God and the universe by upholding an actual dualism and not simply a qualified dualism. This may surprise many in the West. Since, as explained by Deepak Sarma, Madhva's School of Vedanta has been frequently overlooked, the misconception and false generalization that "[a]ll Hindus are monists and want to merge with the divine" is a commonly held Western understanding of Hinduism.[58]

According to traditional accounts of Madhva's life, he was educated by a student of Shankara who taught him the world is only an illusion (*maya*) and does not, therefore, really exist. Believing that the world does exist, Madhva ceased being a student of Shankara's philosophy and formed his own school. According to Madhva, in order to be saved (*moksa*), it is necessary for human beings to be freed from the wheel of reincarnation and suffering. On this point, Madhva was in agreement with Shankara. However, he differed in that he rejected that salvation consists in being totally absorbed into God, a position that Ramanuja also held. In contrast, Madhva maintained that after a person is saved, they retain their individuality and difference from God. This salvation is obtained by study and meditation, but only for those who are preordained by God.[59]

---

[58] Deepak Sarma, *An Introduction to Madhva Vedanta* (Burlington: Ashgate Publishing Co., 2003), ix.

[59] Christian von Dehsen, *Philosophers and Religious Leaders: An Encyclopedia of People who Changed the World* (Chicago: Fitzroy Dearborn, 1999), 118.

Madhva's position is closest, but not equivalent, to the Catholic position on unity and diversity with respect to the Creator and creature as clearly asserted in 1215 by the Fourth Lateran Council:

> When, therefore, the Truth prays to the Father for those faithful to him saying I wish that *they may be one in us just as we are one*, this word one mean for the faithful a union of love in grace, and for the divine persons a unity of identity in nature, as the Truth say elsewhere, *You must be perfect as your heavenly Father is perfect*, as if he were to say more plainly, *You must be perfect* in the perfection of grace, *just as your Father is perfect* in the perfection that is his by nature, each in his own way. For between creator and creature there can be noted no similarity so great that a greater dissimilarity cannot be seen between them.[60]

This passage from the Fourth Lateran Council has frequently been cited in reference to the Catholic concept of the Analogy of Being. As explained by St. Thomas Aquinas, the created world is related to God by an analogy of being called an analogy of attribution. According to this analogy of attribution, God is the primary instance of being while all else is a secondary analogate of being. In other words, the relationship between God and his creation is not B is to G-C where being is B and G an C represent God and

---

[60] Norman P. Tanner, *Decrees of the Ecumenical Councils*, Volume I (Washington, DC: Georgetown University Press, 1990), 232.

his creation. This would make being more fundamental than God himself. Neither is the relationship of God and creation G=C. This is monism. Instead, God's essence (His *whatness* from the Latin verb *esse* meaning to be) is his existence (*esse ipse subsistens*), and the essence of anything else (*esse commune*) does not necessarily indicate it exists. This means that God *is* being (*esse*) while we, along with all of creation, only *have* being (*esse commune*).[61]

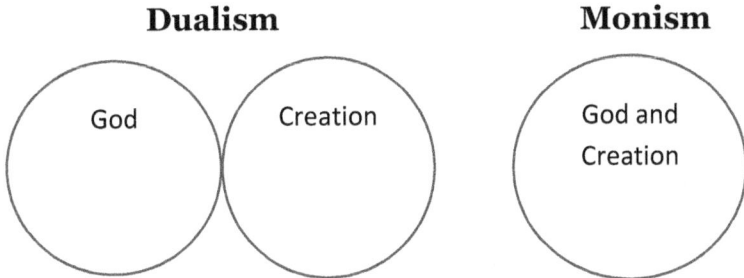

~ Christ as the Concrete Analogy of Being ~

"Since the person of the Logos is the ultimate union of divine and created being, it must

---

[61] *Esse ipse subsistence* means that God's being (essence/whatness) is by itself existing and is the cause of all else that exists (*esse commune*). Esse commune but depends on God for existence. It does so by participating in perfections of God but not in God's essence. Thomas Joseph White, *The Analogy of Being: Invention of the Antichrist or the Wisdom of God?* (Grand Rapids: Wm. B. Eerdmans, 2011), 231.

constitute the final proportion [*Mass*] between the two and hence must be the 'concrete *analogia entis*' itself. However, it must not in any way overstep this analogy in the direction of identity."[62] ~ Hans Urs von Balthasar

Quiz 3 for Chapter 3

1-3. Define the following terms: *Vedas*, *Vedanta*, and *Upanishads*.

1.

2.

3.

4-6. Explain Shankara's absolute monism or non-Dualism. Include the following terms and define them: Atman and Brahman.

7-9. Explain Ramanuja's Qualified non-Dualism. Include the following terms and define them: qualities, and God.

---

[62] Hans Urs von Balthasar, *Theo-Drama*, Volume 3: Dramatis Personae: Persons in Christ, trans. Graham Harrison (San Francisco: Ignatius Press, 1992), 221.

10-12. Explain Madhva's Dualism. Include in your explanation how he understood what happens to the individual soul when it is saved (*moksa*).

13-16. In reference to Shankara, Ramanuja, and Madhva explain the Catholic Analogy of Being.

Chapter 4: Yoga Hinduism

Introduction

As mentioned previously, there are six schools that are considered to be part of orthodox Hinduism: Vedanta, Yoga, Samkhya, Nyaya, Vaisheshika, and Mimamsa. We have already surveyed the most dominant of these six schools, Vedanta Hinduism. In this chapter we will study the Samkhya and Yoga schools of Hinduism that are well-known in the West and which are part of all Hindu schools.[63] We will begin with Samkhya Hinduism since many teachings of this school have been preserved in Yoga. Currently, the ancient Samkha School, dating back to c. 500 BC, has few followers. The introduction to Samkhya will be followed by focusing on Patanjali, who is considered the founder of the Yoga School since is he credited with putting into practice Samkhya theory. Finally, we will conclude with Hatha Yoga, which is a development of but one aspect of Patanjali's Yoga practices.

---

[63] Grant Hardy, *Great Minds of the Eastern Intellectual Tradition*, Lectures 1-18 (Chantilly: The Teaching Company, 2011), 177.

Samkhya

According to tradition, the Samkhya school of Hinduism was begun by Kapila around 500 BC. Its most important text is the *Samkhya Karika* written by Ishvarakrishna (c. 200 AD). The *Samkhya Karika* reduces all of existence to two primary categories: matter (*prakriti*) and spirit (*purusha*). Spirit, teaches the *Samkhya Karika*, is made up of an infinite number of souls. The individual Karma of each soul attracts matter around it which then forms into various bodies according to the type of Karma to which it is drawn. Only by meditation can a soul be freed from attracting matter. For this to occur, though, even the idea of an individual self-reflective mind needs to be abandoned in order for the soul to rest in an inactive, pure (*sattva*) state.[64]

It is important to note that Samkhya's dualism is essentially non-theistic since the school maintains that existence consists of only an infinite number of souls and matter. Samkhya spirit-good and body-bad dualistic spirituality is even more evident in its belief that the limbs of the physical body bind the soul to the suffering of this world while the intellect and soul tend toward the peaceful, pure realm of inaction.[65]

The Samkhya view of matter differs tremendously from the biblical notion of the goodness of matter and

---

[64] Constance Jones, and James D. Ryan, *Encyclopedia of Hinduism* (New York: Infobase Publishing, 2007), 379; Gerald James Larson, *Classical Sāṃkhya: An Interpretation of Its History and Meaning* (), 8-9, 12

[65] Jones and Ryan, 379.

from the Christian doctrine of the incarnation. By becoming incarnate, Jesus Christ saves us through the body and not apart from the body. Another significant difference between Samkhya and Christianity is contained in the teachings from the Ecumenical Council of Vienne (1311-1312). This council clearly asserts it is "erroneous and contrary to the truth of the catholic faith every doctrine or proposition rashly asserting that the substance of the rational or intellectual soul is not of itself and essentially the form of the human body...."[66] Below are key excerpts from *Samkhya Karika* by Ishvarakrishna. As these passages indicate, the fundamental purpose of matter is to set free the spirit from its entrapment. This occurs when the individual soul ceases being actively conscious of its existence by resting in a pure state of isolation.

~ Teachings from the *Samkya Karika* ~

58
As (in) the world (a man) engages in actions for the sake of the cessation of a desire; so also does the *prakriti* [matter] function for the sake of the release of the *purusha* [soul].[67]

64
Thus, from the study (or analysis) of the principles

---

[66] Norman P. Tanner, *Decrees of the Ecumenical Councils*, Volume I (Washington, DC: Georgetown University Press, 1990), 361.

[67] Larson, 273.

(*tattvas*), the "knowledge" (or salvation-knowledge) arises, "I am not (conscious); (consciousness) does not belong to me; the "I" is not (conscious) (and this "knowledge") is complete because free from error, pure and solitary (*kevala*).[68]

68
With the cessation of prakriti due to its purpose having been accomplished, (the *purusha*) on attaining separation from the body, attains isolation (*kaivalya*) which is both certain and final.[69]

Patanjali: Founder of Yoga

Little is known for certain about the life of Patanjali, the founder of Yoga. According to tradition, he wrote the *Mahabhashya* and the *Yoga Sutra*. Scholars, though, have determined that it is not possible for both of these works to be have been written by Patanjali since the former is dated to c. 200 BC while the latter dates to c. 200 AD.[70] The more recent work attributed to Patanjali, the *Yoga Sutra*, is the foundational document of the Yoga school. These sutras present a practical system of obtaining the Samkhya school's goal of freeing the soul from its

---

[68] Larson, 274.
[69] Larson, 275.
[70] Jones and Ryan, *Encyclopedia of Hinduism*, 327, 514.

captivity to matter.[71]

The *Yoga Sutra* is divided into four books. Book 1 discusses the importance of calming the motions of the mind in order to obtain the goal of motionless peace. Book 2 details in eight "branches" practical ways for a practitioner to be liberated. Book 3 describes meditation. According to the Yoga Sutra, the highest degree of mental concentration is when the mind rests without any object. Book 4 concludes the Yoga Sutras with philosophy.[72] A summary of the eight branches is provided below.[73]

Sanskrit Name	Translation	Description
1. Yama	Restraint	Avoid acts that are harmful: non-violence, sexual restraint, no lying, no stealing, no hoarding
2. Niyama	Observance	Doing acts that are beneficial:
3. Asana	Postures	Having a comfortable, right posture when meditating. .
4. Pranayama	Regulation of	Breathing

---

[71] Jones and Ryan, 379.
[72] Jones and Ryan, 327, 514.
[73] B. Ravikanth, *Yoga Sutras of Patanjali: The Nature of the Mind, the Universe, and the True Self* ([S.I.]:Sanskrit Works, 2012), 139-153.

	Breath	properly in order to calm the mind.
5. Pratyahara	Withdrawal of the Senses	Detachment from the senses.
6. Dharana	Focusing the Mind	Focusing the mental powers on a specific object.
7. Dhyana	Meditation	Sustaining the focus of the mental powers on a specific object.
8. Samadhi	Absorption	Absorption in contemplation.

The great Saint Teresa of Avila (1515-1582) once mistakenly thought that the highest degree of prayer is to be totally absorbed in contemplation where all objects, including the humanity of Christ, are put aside. In acknowledging her error she wrote:

~ Christo-Centric Prayer of St. Teresa ~

When I began to gain some experience of supernatural prayer-I mean of the Prayer of Quiet-I tried to put aside everything corporeal, though I dared not lift up my soul, for, being always so wicked, I saw that to do this would be presumption. But I thought I was experiencing the presence of God, as proved to be true, and I contrived to remain with Him in a state of recollection. This type of prayer, if God has a part in it, is full delight, and brings great joy. And in view of the advantage I was deriving from it and the pleasure it was bringing me, no one could have made me return to meditation on the Humanity – on the contrary, this really seemed to me a hindrance. O Lord of my soul and my Good, Jesus Christ crucified! Never once do I recall this opinion which I held without a feeling of pain: I believe I was committing an act of high treason, though I committed it in ignorance. ...This withdrawal from the corporeal must doubtless be good, since it is advised by such spiritual people, but my belief is that it must be practiced only when the soul is very proficient: until then, it is clear, the Creator must be sought through creatures. All this has to do with the grace which the Lord bestows on every soul: into that matter I will not enter. What I should like to make clear is that Christ's most sacred Humanity must not be reckoned among these corporeal objects.[74]

Hatha Yoga

Hatha Yoga further developed the third limb from the Yoga Sutras. The purpose is two-fold: to prepare one for meditation and to keep the body healthy. Below are some examples of various yoga postures called asanas.[75] Many in the West erroneously mistake

---

[74] Teresa of Avila, *The Life of Teresa of Avila*, trans. E. Allison Peers (New York: Doubleday 1991), 210-211, 213.

[75] B. Ravikanth, *Yoga Sutras of Patanjali: The Nature of the Mind, the Universe, and the True Self* ([S.I.]:Sanskrit Works, 2012), 154.

this one aspect of Yoga with Yoga in its entirety.

---

[76] OrenBochman, "Virabhadrasana I or Warrior Pose I," photograph, https://commons.wikimedia.org/wiki/File%3AVirabhadrasana_I_-_Warrior_Pose_I.jpg, (accessed July 3, 2015).
[77] lululemon athletica, "Warrior II," photograph, https://commons.wikimedia.org/wiki/File%3AWarrior_II.jpg, (accessed July 3, 2015).
[78] Drchirag patel, "Tuladandasana or warrior pose III," photograph, https://commons.wikimedia.org/wiki/File%3ATuladandasana.jpg, (accessed July 3, 2015).
[79] Tia Tran, "Yoga in the Sivananda Yoga Tradition in La Mesa, Colombia," photograph, https://commons.wikimedia.org/wiki/File%3ACaptura_de_pantalla_2011-05-01_a_las_12.13.14.png, (accessed July 3, 2015).
[80] Kenngurn, "Parivrtta Baddha Parsvakonasana by Nina Mel, Yoga Teacher," photograph, https://www.commons.wikimedia.org/wiki/File%3AParivrtta-Baddha-

Eastern Civilization from a Catholic Viewpoint

Parsvakonasana_Yoga-Asana_Nina-Mel.jpg, (accessed July 3, 2015).

[81] lululemon athelica, "Hanumanasana," photograph, https://commons.wikimedia.org/wiki/File%3AHanumanasana_-_Hanuman's_Posture_-_in_Diagonal_View.jpg, (accessed July 3, 2015).

[82] lululemon athletica, "Plank Pose," photograph, https://commons.wikimedia.org/wiki/File%3AYoga_PLank.jpg, (accessed July 3, 2015).

[83] Joseph RENGER, "Yoga postures Ado-muka-shvanasana," photograph, https://commons.wikimedia.org/wiki/File%3AAdo-muka-shvanasana.jpg, (accessed July 3, 2015).

[84] Elsie Escobar, http://elsiesyogakula.com, "*mālāsana*, garland pose," photograph, https://commons.wikimedia.org/wiki/File%3AMalasana.jpg, (accessed July 3, 2015).

⁸⁵ Iveto, "Child's Pose (relaxation)," photograph, https://commons.wikimedia.org/wiki/File%3ABalasana.JPG, (accessed July 3, 2015).

⁸⁶ Drchirag patel, "Peacock Pose," photograph, https://commons.wikimedia.org/wiki/File%3APeacock_pose.jpg, (accessed July 3, 2015).

⁸⁷ Kennguru, "Chakrasana by Nina Mel, Yoga Teacher," photograph, https://commons.wikimedia.org/wiki/File%3AChakrasana_Yoga-Asana_Nina-Mel.jpg, (accessed July 3, 2015).

⁸⁸ Kenngurn, "Parivrtta Baddha Parsvakonasana by Nina Mel, Yoga Teacher," photograph, https://www.commons.wikimedia.org/wiki/File%3AParivrtta-Baddha-Parsvakonasana_Yoga-Asana_Nina-Mel.jpg, (accessed July 3, 2015).

⁸⁹ Joseph RENGER, "Yoga postures sarvangasana," photograph, https://commons.wikimedia.org/wiki/File%3ASarvangasana.jpg, (accessed July 3, 2015).

⁹⁰ Joseph RENGER, "Yoga postures Shirshasana," photograph, https://commons.wikimedia.org/wiki/File%3AShirshasana.jpg, (accessed July 3, 2015).

⁹¹ Joseph Renger, "Yoga postures Shavasana," photograph, https://commons.wikimedia.org/wiki/File%3AShavasana.jpg, (accessed July 3, 2015).

Quiz 4 for Chapter 4

1-4 According to the Samkhya school of Hinduism what are the two primary categories of existence? Also, is this school theistic? Why or why not?

1.

2.

3.

4.

5-6. According to Samkhya why and how does matter form into bodies? In addition, how can a soul be freed from matter?

5.

6.

7-9. Describe in three ways how the Samkhya's view of matter differs from Catholicism.

7.

8.

9.

10. Listed below are the eight limbs from the *Yoga Sutra*. Explain in five ways how these teachings are

similar and very different from Catholic teaching. Include in your answer reference to Saint Teresa of Avila's teaching on contemplation.

Sanskrit Name	**Translation**	**Description**
1. Yama	Restraint	Avoid acts that are harmful: non-violence, sexual restraint, no lying, no stealing, no hoarding
2. Niyama	Observance	Doing acts that are beneficial:
3. Asana	Postures	Having a comfortable, right posture when meditating. .
4. Pranayama	Regulation of Breath	Breathing properly in order to calm the mind.
5. Pratyahara	Withdrawal of the Senses	Detachment from the senses.
6. Dharana	Focusing the Mind	Focusing the mental powers on a specific object.

| 7. Dhyana | Meditation | Sustaining the focus of the mental powers on a specific object. |
| 8. Samadhi | Absorption | Absorption in contemplation. |

[92]

---

[92] B. Ravikanth, *Yoga Sutras of Patanjali: The Nature of the Mind, the Universe, and the True Self* ([S.I.]: Sanskrit Works, 2012), 139-153.

Chapter 5: Indian Extreme Pluralism and Persian (Iranian) Dualism

Introduction

In previous chapters you were introduced to monistic and dualistic interpretations of the *Vedas*, which Hinduism considers as sacred text. In this chapter we will examine a few similar, but non-Hindu, Eastern religions: Jainism, Zoroastrianism, and Manichaeism.

Jainism and Pluralism

Vardamana (c. 540-468 B.C.) was the founder of Jainism. He was considered to be a member of India's Kshatria warrior class. After he chose the life of an ascetic and renounced his privileged state, he attracted followers. His followers called him Mahavira, which means Great Hero.[93] Unlike monistic

---

[93] Helmuth von Glasenapp, *Jainism: An Indian Religion of Salvation* (Delhi: Motilal Banarsidass Publishers, 1999.), 29.

Brahmanism, in which difference is an illusion, Mahavira taught that difference is actual. It is so actual that every creature has an individual soul. His doctrine of a plurality of souls led him to teach an extreme form of non-violence. He even considered killing mosquitoes a forbidden violent act. In time, he also held that wearing clothes entailed participation in forbidden violent acts since the production of clothes necessarily causes unwarranted pain to plant souls. Not surprisingly, following his extreme beliefs his life ended tragically. Naked and hungry, he starved to death.[94]

Jainism also developed its affirmation of real pluralism by asserting, in their doctrine of Manifold Predictions, that there are many variations of truth. In other words, truth is relative, but not in the sense that truth does not exist. A story that illustrates this pluralistic concept of truth is contained in the following Jain story.

~ Jain Story of the Elephant and the Blind Man ~

An elephant was once brought in to a village, home to six blind men. None of them had ever encountered an elephant. Wanting to experience this creature the six of them decided to meet the animal. Upon arriving the first took hold of the elephant's leg and claimed that the animal is like a tree. Another grabbed hold of the elephant's tail

---

[94] Grant Hardy, *Great Minds of the Eastern Intellectual Tradition*, Lectures 1-18 (Chantilly: The Teaching Company, 2011), 34-37.

and said it's like a rope. The third touched the elephant's tusk and asserted that it's like a pillar. Upon feeling the elephant's ear, the fourth exclaimed that it's like a fan. The fifth felt the elephant's belly and described it like a wall, while the sixth, running his hand down the elephant's trunk, said it's like a branch. Since each of them were convinced they were right they started arguing until a sage walked by and calmed them down. Once peace was restored, the sage affirmed that all six blind men spoke the truth since each one was feeling a different part of the elephant.[95]

[96]

A principle reason for this pluralistic concept of

---

[95] This story is based on the following version. "Elephant and the Blind Man," Jain World, http://www.jainworld.com/education/stories25.asp, (accessed June 16, 2015).

[96] Author Illustrator unknown, "Blind Men and Elephant," illustration, https://commons.wikimedia.org/wiki/File%3ABlind_men_and_elephant3.jpg (accessed June 16, 2015).

truth is that Jainism, along with other Indian philosophies and religions, rejects the belief of a creating intellect responsible for bringing forth the world. In Jainism, the universe has no beginning nor end, and, therefore, no creator. Instead, the universe is identified with a multitude of transformations and creations by the billions of souls that constitute it, each with its unique Karma.[97]

In order for the soul to transform itself and to create beneficial cosmic effects it needs to grow in good karma. Such growth is principally obtained by following the five basic vows of Jainism listed below. Jain and monks and nuns observe these vows to a higher degree, for example by living out a celibate live, owning nothing, practicing absolute non-violence even in desire, etc.

1. Nonviolence (*ahimsa*): to refrain from directly and deliberately taking the life of any animal or human being.
2. Truthfulness (*satya*): to tell the truth and to engage in honest business practices.
3. Non-stealing (*asteya*): not to steal.
4. Sexual chastity (*brahmacarya*): to refrain from committing marital infidelity and to avoid pre-marital sexual activity.
5. Non-attachment (*aparigraha*): to avoid being possessive and materialistic.[98]

---

[97] Jeffrey D. Long, *Jainism: An Introduction* (London: I.B. Tauris, 2009), 83-85.
[98] Long, 101.

Zoroastrianism

Zoroastrianism differs from both Brahmanism monism and Jainism pluralism. For Zoroastrians, the world is essentially dualistic. Its two realities and actual sources for all that exists are goodness and evil. Instead of understanding evil as an absence of due good, which Catholicism teaches, Zoroastrianism teaches that goodness and evil are equal forces enmeshed in an eternal, cosmic struggle. Ahura Mazda is the Zoroastrian god of goodness while Angra Mainya is the god of evil. Both of these gods are held to be uncreated and, from this perspective, equal to each other. Zoroastrians only worship Ahura Mazda out of faith that even though he is not all powerful, as Christianity teaches God is, he will eventually defeat Angra Mainya. This religion and philosophy was founded by the Persian priest Zarathustra, also known by his Greek name Zoroaster. It is not clear when he lived, but it was most likely between 1400-1000 BC. [99]

Seventeen hymns, called Gathas, are attributed to Zarathustra. These make up the Zoroastrians' most sacred texts. In the *Ahununvaiti Gatha*, Zarathustra describes an essentially dualistic world.

~ Zarathustra on Good and Evil ~

3. In the beginning there were two
    primal spirits,
Twins spontaneously active,

---

[99] Hardy, 150-154.

These are the Good and the Evil, in thought,
and in word, and in deed.
Between these two, let the wise choose aright.
Be good, not base!

4. And when these Twin Spirits came together at first,
They established Life and the Denial of Life;
And so shall it be till the world will last.
The worst existence shall be the lot of the followers of evil,
And the state of Best-Consciousness be the reward of the righteous.

5. Of these Twin Spirits, the Evil one chooses doing
the worst,
While the most bountiful Holy Spirit of Goodness,
clothing itself in the imperishable heavens,
chooses Truth and Righteousness.
And so will those who would please Ahura Mazda
with righteous deeds, performed with faith in Truth.

6. Between these two Spirits the

Demon-worshipers
could not discern aright.
To them Deception came at the time
    of decision,
And they chose the Worst Mind.
With violence then they rushed
    together,
Life, in the world, to destroy.

7. And to support this life comes
    Armaity, the spirit of
Benevolence and Right-mindedness.
Together with the Spirit of Holy
    Power, the Good Mind, and
    Truth,
That the soul, passing through the
    test of truth,
shall be with Thee, O Lord.

8. And when there cometh the
    ultimate retribution
for the evil ones,
Then, at Thy Ordinance, shall the
    Good Mind
establish the Kingdom of Heaven, O
    Ahura!
For those who will deliver Untruth
    into the hands of Truth.

9. So may we be like those making
    the world progress
toward perfection;

May Mazda and the Divine Spirits
    help us and
guide our efforts through Truth;
For a thinking man is where Wisdom
    is at home.

10. Then truly cometh the blow of
    destruction upon Untruth;
While those of good renown shall be
    received in
the promised abode,
The blessed abode of the Good Mind,
    of Truth, and
of the Wise Lord.

11. O ye mortals, mark these
    commandments,
The commandments the Wise Lord
    has given for
happiness and for pain:
Long suffering for the doer of Evil,
    and bliss
for the follower of Truth,
The illumination of salvation for the
    Righteous ever after.[100]

---

[100] "Ahunuvaiti Gatha, Yasna 30, Zarathustra, http://www.zarathushtra.com/z/gatha/dji/yasna30.htm, (accessed June 18, 2015).

Mani and Manichaeism

In the third century AD, a Gnostic and quasi-Christian form of Zoroastrianism was developed by the Persian, Mani (c. 216-274 A.D.). The religion he founded is known as Manichaeism. This is the religion that the great Church Father St. Augustine (354-430 AD) believed in and practiced before converting to Catholicism. In his *Against the Fundamental Epistle of Manichaeus*, Augustine rejects Mani's claim of the opening verse of Mani's *Fundamental Epistle*. Here, Mani claims that he is "an apostle of Jesus Christ, by the providence of God the Father."[101] Mani cannot be a true apostle of Jesus Christ, argues Augustine, because his teachings are heretical. Borrowing from Zoroastrian dualism, Mani teaches in *The Gospel of the Prophet Mani*:

> Light and Dark, Good and Evil, are the two opposite and coeternal Sources of all that is. They are mingled together when the ambition of Evil to possess the Light had to be countered by God sending a Light-Spark from Himself, the conscious Soul, down into Matter to uplift and purify the

---

[101] St. Augustine, "Against the Fundamental Epistle of Manichaeus," chap. 5, New Advent, http://www.newadvent.org/fathers/1405.htm, (accessed June 18, 2015). New Advent cites the following. Translated by Richard Stothert. From Nicene and Post-Nicene Fathers, First Series, Vol. 4. Edited by Philip Schaff. (Buffalo, NY: Christian Literature Publishing Co., 1887.) Revised and edited for New Advent by Kevin Knight. <http://www.newadvent.org/fathers/1405.htm>.

Light therein entangled everywhere. Manifested in five-fold Potencies, or 'Sons', perfectly reflected in the five aspects of the human mind, God's 'Living Spirit' fashioned the universe as a means to separate gradually these primal Sources. This story of the One Soul is repeated by every individual Soul aspiring to return to its lost Kingdom of the Light near God, and aided thereto by Divine Outpourings and the human Messengers of the Light who found religions.[102]

Augustine counters this excessively dualistic assertion on good and evil by defining evil as only existing in good and as an absence of good that ought to be present. In chapter thirty-four of *Against the Fundamental Epistle of Manichaeus,* Augustine argues:

~ Nature Cannot Be without Some Good: The Manichæans Dwell upon the Evils ~

But perhaps you will say that these evils cannot be removed from the natures, and must therefore be considered natural. The question at present is not what can be taken away, and what cannot; but it certainly helps to a clear perception that these natures, as far as they are natures, are good, when we see that the good things can be thought of without these evil things, while without these good

---

[102] Duncan Greenlees, *The Gospel of the Prophet Mani* (Adyar: The Theosophical Publishing House, 2007), vii.

things no nature can be conceived of. I can conceive of waters without muddy commotion; but without settled continuity of parts no material form is an object of thought or of sensation in any way. Therefore even these muddy waters could not exist without the good which was the condition of their material existence. As to the reply that these evil things cannot be taken from such natures, I rejoin that neither can the good things be taken away. Why, then, should you call these things natural evils, on account of the evil things which you suppose cannot be taken away, and yet refuse to call them natural good things, on account of the good things which, as has been proved, cannot be taken away?[103]

Continuing his argument in chapter thirty-six, titled *The Source of Evil or of Corruption of Good*, Augustine further asserts:

After thus inquiring what evil is, and learning that it is not nature, but against nature, we must next inquire whence it is. If Manichæus had done this, he might have escaped falling into the snare of these serious errors. Out of time and out of order, he began with inquiring into the origin of evil, without first asking what evil was; and so his inquiry led him only to the reception of foolish fancies, of which the mind, much fed by the bodily

---

[103] St. Augustine, "Against the Fundamental Epistle of Manichaeus," chap. 35.

senses, with difficulty rids itself. Perhaps, then, someone, desiring no longer argument, but delivery from error, will ask, Whence is this corruption which we find to be the common evil of good things which are not incorruptible? ... For to answer in a word the question, whence is corruption? It is hence, because these natures that are capable of corruption were not begotten by God, but made by Him out of nothing; and as we already proved that those natures are good, no one can say with propriety that they were not good as made by God. If it is said that God made them perfectly good, it must be remembered that the only perfect good is God Himself, the maker of those good things.[104]

Quiz 5 for Chapter 5

1. Contrast Brahman monism with Jainism.

2. Contrast Catholic doctrine with Jainism. (Hint – creation)

3-4. Why does Jainism teach non-violence? Near the end of Mahavira's life what did this founder of Jainism do in order to be as non-violent as possible?

---

[104] St. Augustine, chap. 36.

3.

4.

5-7. List three of the five vows of Jainism.

5.

6.

7.

8-9. Contrast Zoroastrianism with Brahman monism and Jainism's pluralism.

8.

9.

10-12. Explain how Augustine dismisses the Zoroastrian element of Mani's teaching on good and evil.

10.

11.

12.

Chapter 6: Hindu Gods - Monotheism and Pantheism

Introduction

Hindu thought on the relationship of the one to the many is expressed in popular devotion by worship of many gods. It is popularly held that there are 330 million Hindu gods.[105] This does not mean, as the following story from the Brihadâranyaka Upanishad illustrates, that worshippers of these gods are strict polytheists. Instead, since the gods are understood as manifestations of the divine, Hindus who believe in the gods can be monotheistic or pantheistic. (Some Hindus are even atheistic). The type of God or types of Gods a Hindu adheres to depends on the degree he accepts a dualistic understanding of reality, or a pluralistic view of reality, or a non-dualistic concept. If the latter, then even if the Hindu appears to be worshipping many gods he is actually only worshipping one God who is manifested in many different forms including within the devotee himself

---

[105] Priya Hemenway, *Hindu Gods: The Spirit of the Divine* (San Francisco: Chronicle Books, 2003), 19.

who also is God.

~ How Many Hindu Gods are There? ~

From the *Brihadâranyaka Upanishad*

> 1. Then Vidagdha Sâkalya asked him 2: 'How many gods are there, O Yâgñavalkya?' He replied with this very Nivid 3: 'As many as are mentioned in the Nivid of the hymn of praise addressed to the Visvedevas, viz. three and three hundred, three and three thousand 4.'
> 'Yes,' he said, and asked again: 'How many gods are there really, O Yâgñavalkya?'
> 'Thirty-three,' he said.
> 'Yes,' he said, and asked again: 'How many gods are there really, O Yâgñavalkya?'
> 'Six,' he said.
> 'Yes,' he said, and asked again: 'How many gods are there really, O Yâgñavalkya?'
> 'Three,' he said.
> 'Yes,' he said, and asked again: 'How many gods are there really, O Yâgñavalkya?'
> 'Two,' he said.
> 'Yes,' he said, and asked again: 'How many gods are there really, O Yâgñavalkya?'
> 'One and a half (adhyardha),' he said.
> 'Yes,' he said, and asked again: 'How many gods are there really, O Yâgñavalkya?'

'One,' he said.[106]

Avatars of Vishnu - Singapore[107]

---

[106] "Brihadâranyaka Upanishad," trans. Max Muller, III. 9. 1, p. 139-140, Sacred Texts, http://www.sacred-texts.com/hin/sbe15/sbe15072.htm, (accessed July 15, 2015).

[107] Steve Jurvetson, "Singapore. Statue of Krishna as Vishnu in his Vishwarupa (Universal form). Krishna showed his Vishwarupa to Arjuna, during the narration of the Bhagavad Gita before the Mahabharata war," photograph, https://commons.wikimedia.org/wiki/File:Avatars_of_Vishnu.jpg, (accessed July 15, 2015).

Divine Manifestations of Brahma[108]

Hindu Mythology

Hindu mythology is contained in a variety of works. The *Puranas* (written 300-1600 AD) traces the origins of the Hindu Gods and Goddesses in the section titled "Vayu Purana".[109] Two other works that describe the gods, but in epic form, are the *Mahabharata* and the *Ramayana* which are comparable in status to the Greek *Iliad* and *Odyssey*. A very popular story of the Gods comes from the *Mahabharata* and is called the *Bhagavad-gita*.

This story relates the interaction of Prince Arjuna with Krishna, an earthly manifestation of the God

---

[108] Author not listed, "A hand-colored engraving of Brahma," photograph, https://commons.wikimedia.org/wiki/File:Brahma_1820.jpg, (accessed July 15, 2015).

[109] "The Vayu Purana," Dharmashetra.com, http://www.dharmakshetra.com/literature/puranas/Vayu%20Purana.htm, (accessed July 28, 2015).

Vishnu.[110] (As a manifestation of a God, Vishnu is called an avatar. The word avatar comes from the Sanskrit word *avatarana* from *ava-* "off, down" plus *tarati* "crosses over.[111] In Hinduism, an avatar is a God who takes on human form on earth.) The avatar Krishna and Prince Arjuna relate primarily by way of conversation. Their dialogue centers on Prince Arjuna's unwillingness to fight in a battle in which members of his family are represented on both sides. Eventually, Krishna convinces Prince Arjuna to fulfill his duty of fighting as a warrior. The battle in the *Bhagavad-gita* is typically interpreted spiritually as signifying the common inner struggle over issues that are not black and white but uncertain and unclear.[112] In the last chapter of the *Bhagavad-gita* Krishna insists that Prince Arjuna fulfills his duty as a warrior of the Pandavas in their war against the Kurus by asserting:

> Better thine own work is, though done with fault, than doing others' work, ev'n excellently. He shall not fall in sin who fronts the task set him by Nature's hand! Let no man leave His natural duty, Prince! Though it bear blame! For every work hath

---

[110] Mark W. Muesse, *Great world Religions: Hinduism* (Chantilly: The Great Courses, 2003), 42.

[111] "Avatar," Online Etymology Dictionary, http://www.etymonline.com/index.php?allowed_in_frame=0&search=avatar&searchmode=none (accessed October 4, 2015).

[112] Muesse, 38-40; "The Bhagavad-Gita," Project Gutenberg, http://www.gutenberg.org/files/2388/2388-h/2388-h.htm#chap18, (accessed July 28, 2015).

blame, as every flame is wrapped in smoke! Only that man attains Perfect surcease of work whose work was wrought with mind unfettered, soul wholly subdued, desires for ever dead, results renounced.[113]

Persuaded, Prince Arjuna brings his conversation with Krishna to an end by surrendering his will to accomplishing his warrior role with, "Trouble and ignorance are gone! The Light hath come unto me, by Thy favor, Lord! Now am I fixed! My doubt is fled away! According to Thy word, so will I do!"[114]

A Few Popular Hindu Gods

The Vayu Purana section of the *Puranas* traces the origin of the Creator god Brahma to an original divine essence called Brahman that is identified as nothing material. Carefully read the passage below that describes the Brahman. Do you think that it is describing the absence of anything? It seems that instead of describing nothingness it is actually describing something, otherwise how could nothing be the origin of the universe? Catholics believe that God is nothing material since He belongs to the spiritual order and is its essence. This spiritual

---

[113] "The Bhagavad-Gita," Chapter XVIII (accessed July 28, 2015).

[114] "The Bhagavad-Gita," Chapter VIII (accessed July 28, 2015).

someone caused nothing material to be something.¹¹⁵ In Judaism and in Christianity this something that cannot be felt, seen, or smelt, since it is not physical, is identified as God who created all that exists.

~ Creation ~

In the beginning, there was nothing in the universe. The brahman (the divine essence) alone was everywhere. The brahman had neither colour nor scent, it could not be felt or touched. It had no origin, no beginning or no end. The brahman was constant and it was the origin of everything that was destined to be in the universe and the universe was shrouded in darkness.

When it was time for creation to begin, the brahman divided itself into three. The first part became Brahma, the creator of the universe. The second part was Vishnu, the preserver of the universe. And the third part was Shiva, the destroyer.

At the time of creation, water appeared in the universe and the water was everywhere. In the

---

[115] Robert Spitzer, "Teaching Science and Faith – Conflict or Confluence? For High School Science and Religion Teachers," Institute for Theological Encounter with Science and Technology and the Magis Center, http://mp125118.cdn.mediaplatform.com/125118/wc/mp/4000/5592/5599/40716/Lobby/default.htm, (accessed February 28, 2015).

water was created a golden (hiranya) egg (anda) that floated like a gigantic bubble. Brahma was born inside the egg. Since garbha means womb, Brahma came to be known as Hiranyagarbha. Since he effectively created (bhu) himself (svayam), he is also referred to as Svayambhu.

Brahma had four faces.

Also inside the egg were all the worlds (lokas) that would be created, in embryonic form. The earth was there, with its land, mountains, oceans and rivers. The moon, the sun, the stars and the planets were there. Also present were gods, demons, humans and other living beings who would be created.

This was the original creation of the universe (sarga).

But at the end of one of Brahma's days, a minor destruction takes place. The universe is once again flooded with water during Brahma's night. Brahma, Vishnu and Shiva are not however destroyed. Each of Brahma's days is known as a kalpa (cycle). Thus, a minor destruction takes place at the end of every kalpa. When a new day dawns for Brahma, creation begins afresh. This periodical process of destruction (pralaya) and recreation is known as pratisarga.[116]

The passage above refers to the three principal Gods that, along with Brahma, originated out of brahman. The triad of Gods is Brahma the creator, Vishnu, the sustainer of life, and Shiva, the destroyer of life. Each one is married to a manifestation of the Mahadevi. The Mahadevi is the Great Goddess. She is married to Brahma as the Devi Sarasvati, to Shiva as the Devi Sati, and Vishnu as the Devi Lakshmi.[117]

The most terrifying Devi is Kali, who also marries Shiva, the God of destruction. Below is picture of Kali stomping on her husband Shiva. Notice that the action, in this case destructive action, is associated with the feminine while the masculine principle, represented by Shiva, is associated with passivity. In Hinduism, the passive masculine principle is known as Siva, and the active, creative power is called Sakti.[118]

---

[116] "The Vayu Purana," Dharmashetra.com, http://www.dharmakshetra.com/literature/puranas/Vayu%20Purana.htm, (accessed July 28, 2015).

[117] "The Vayu Purana," Dharmashetra.com; Muesse, 42.

[118] Muesse, 45-44.

As described by Wolf-Dieter Storl, Kali is "bloodthirsty and cruel.... She is time (kala) that mercilessly devours everything that dared manifest

---

[119] Unidentified photographer, "Kali trampling Shiva. Chromolithograph by R. Varma," photograph, https://commons.wikimedia.org/wiki/File%3AKali_by_R aja_Ravi_Varma.jpg, (accessed July 28, 2015).

itself in the world of existence. She absorbs all, destroys all....She is the sheerest evil for the ego, that sense of personal identity that longs to build itself a monument, give itself some hold, some sort of permanence."[120] Storl continues, though, by explaining the paradoxical devotion that Hindus have for Kali. "In a deeper sense," he writes, "Kali is the loving Mother, who, through the power of time, graciously destroys the monstrous ego-illusion."[121]

One group of devotees of Kali are known as the Thuggees. According to various accounts, at times disputed, these Kali followers honored their goddess by strangling thousands of innocent victims.[122] In the 1820s, when India was under British rule (1858-1947), the British officer William Sleeman was appointed to bring an end to this cult. In doing so he may have exaggerated the threat the Thuggees posed.[123]

Tantrism is another form of devotion to the Goddess and her many forms that is still practiced today. It is divided into two types, left-handed Tantra and right-handed Tantra. The *Tantras* are the sacred texts for both of these worshippers of Kali. Right-handed devotees worship the Goddess without any practices that we would consider shocking. The so-

---

[120] Wolf-Dieter Storl, *Shiva: The Wild God of Power and Ecstasy* (Rochester: Inner Traditions, 2004), 122.

[121] Storl, 123.

[122] Storl, 125.

[123] Storl, 125; Kim A. Wagner, *Thuggee: Banditry and the British in Early Nineteenth-Century India* (New York: Palgrave-Macmillan, 2007), 1, 19, 116.

called left-handed worshippers, however, practice a ritual that is unusual including for many Hindus. The Tantric ritual consists of eating meat, drinking alcohol and engaging in intimate relations in a supervised, controlled environment with those they are not married to all for, they believe, the purpose of attaining enlightenment.[124]

The practices of those devoted to the Devi and her many divine manifestations stem from the belief, implicitly taught by the Upanishads, that ultimately there is no distinction between anything. Difference is but an illusion. Clinging onto difference, especially a sense of one's personal identity, is viewed as the source of all suffering.[125] Is this conviction true? In order to be freed from suffering must we accept that we all are God and the distinction between God and humans, among humans, and between humans and the material world is false?

Catholicism maintains in a convincing manner that the above assertions are false. A modern assertion that is similar to the tendency in Hinduism to reject difference in order to be exalted and enlightened is the premise of Ludwig Feuerbach (1804-1872) who rejected God in order to affirm man. He argued that Christianity, and like religions which maintain that God is essentially different from man by being all knowing, all good, all powerful, all loving, and all beautiful, necessarily means that "man must

---

[124] Muesse, 44-45.
[125] Muesse, 33.

become poor; that God may be all."[126]

Feuerbach's premise, though, assumes that God is a rival, a competitor with human beings.[127] God, as believed by Catholics, is not understood, points out Bishop Barron, as a competitor with creation. Barron explains, "since he is not the supreme being but the very ground of being,"[128] our worship of him allows us, by participating ever more deeply in divine nature (2 Peter 1:4) to be greater than we are, not poorer. We have existence (being) by participating in a being whose essence (what something is) is equal to his existence (that something is). Aquinas teaches God's essence equals his existence, since only He is being that does not need to participate in any other being. We, and the rest of creation, are fundamentally different from God since we have being from God who is the ground of all being.

As the one who maintains all life and existence, God is not a competitor with that which He has created but its sustainer (*creatio continua*). "If," argues Aquinas, "He [God] is not His own existence He will not be essential, but participated being. He will not therefore be the first being-which is absurd.

---

[126] Ludwig Feuerbach, *The Essence of Christianity*, trans. George Eliot (Amherst: Prometheus Books, 1989), 26.

[127] Robert Barron, *Transcript of Catholic Media Conference Opening Keynote Address "Six Suggestions About What Would Make the New Evangelization More Effective,"* June 19, 2013 Denver, Colorodo. Transcribed by The Colorado Catholic Herald, Colorado Springs

[128] Robert Barron, *Catholicism: A Journey to the Heart of the Faith* (New York: Image Books, 2011), 246.

Therefore God is His own existence, and not merely His own essence."[129] Without the essential difference between God and creation nothing would exist since out of nothing comes nothing. God is the non-contingent, non-dependent being who, as someone, called forth existence from nothing. To be exalted, therefore, necessarily entails not denying difference but affirming both difference and similarity, with difference always being greater between God and that which he created.[130] Men and women are saved and grow in being by participating more deeply in the ground of all being who is God, who continually sustains us in existence, and is distinct from us.

Quiz 6 for Chapter 6

1-3. Answer the following question in at least three different ways according to various forms of Hinduism. How many Hindu gods are there?

1.

2.

3.

---

[129] Thomas Aquinas, *Summa Theologica*, trans. Fathers of the Dominican Province (Allen: Christian Classics, 1981), I, q. 3, art. 4.

[130] Reference to Lateran Council IV. Norman P. Tanner, *Decrees of the Ecumenical Councils*, Volume I (Washington, DC: Georgetown University Press, 1990), 232.

4-6. What was Prince Arjuna in the *Bhagavad-gita* struggling with and why? What was his decision and, in your opinion, why did he take this decision?

4.

5.

6.

7-8. The *Vaya Purana* states that in the beginning there was nothing. At the same time, it claims that Brahman, the divine essence, existed. Is this a contradiction? Why or why not?

7.

8.

9-14. Write on the Hindu devotion to the Devi. Include the following terms when writing: Mahadevi, Devi Kali, Shiva, passive, active, and Thuggees.

15-19. According to Catholicism why is the following false? Difference is but an illusion and clinging onto one's identity is the source of suffering. In responding include the following terms: God as a rival, being, participation, difference and similarity.

Chapter 7: Buddha

Introduction

Siddhartha Gautama (563-483 B.C.) was a contemporary of Mahavira, the founder of Jainism. He also was a fellow Indian. Siddhartha, later renamed Buddha, proposed an alternative spiritual path which he considered moderate in comparison with Jainism and other highly ascetical religions. For this reason, Buddha considered his religious path to be a Middle Way that stands between extreme asceticism and hedonism. In studying Buddhism, we will first take a glance at the life of its founder and his confrontation with the reality of suffering. Then, you will be introduced to the Four Noble Truths of Buddhism. We will go deeper in the fourth noble truth by focusing on the eightfold path of ending suffering, which entails a code of ethics adaptable to one's station in life.

Buddha

According to the Indian writer Asvaghosa (c.80-150 AD) in *Acts of the Buddha,* Siddhartha Gautama was born into a royal family called the Sakyas,[131] who ruled in the city of Kapilavastu, located in modern day Nepal. He was slated to inherit his father's kingdom. Despite his father's efforts to shield him from the harsh realities of life and pamper him with sensual pleasures,[132] Siddhartha was confronted with pain and death, including the fleetingness of sexual love which many beautiful women offered to him. He disappointed them, "and the women, having worn their garlands and ornaments in vain, with their graceful arts and endearments all fruitless, concealing their love deep in their hearts, returned to the city with broken hopes."[133] His father, who was hoping to turn his son away from his pursuit of deeper meaning in life through the beauty of women, "could not lie down all that night, like an elephant with an arrow in its heart; but wearied in all sorts of consultation, he and his ministers could find no other means beside these (despised) pleasures to restrain his son's purpose."[134]

As described by Asvaghosa, Siddhartha, "the son of the Śākya king, even though thus tempted by the objects of sense which infatuate others, yielded not to pleasure and felt no delight, like a lion deeply pierced

---

[131] Asvaghosa, *The Buddha-Carita, or Life of the Buddha, or Acts of the Buddha*, ed. Edward B. Cowell supplemented by Anandajoti Bhikkhu with E.H. Johnson's translation of Asvaghosa's work, book I, no. 14, http://ancient-buddhist-texts.net/Texts-and-Translations/Buddhacarita/Buddhacarita.pdf (accessed June 6, 22).

[132] Asvaghosa, book II, no. 25 (accessed June 6, 22).

[133] Asvaghosa, book IV, no. 101 (accessed June 6, 22).

[134] Asvaghosa, book IV, no. 103 (accessed June 6, 22).

in his heart by a poisoned arrow."[135] Deciding that the life his father had in mind for him was vain, he fled to take up the life of an ascetic. According to the Acts of the Buddha, "For six years [Siddhartha], vainly trying to attain merit, practiced self-mortification, performing many rules of abstinence, hard for a man to carry out."[136] At the end of the six years, he deemed his fasting and other ascetical practices as "not the way to passionlessness, nor to perfect knowledge, nor to liberation."[137] He concluded that only through "contemplation are obtained those conditions through which is eventually gained that supreme calm, undecaying, immortal state, which is so hard to be reached."[138]

Then he sat down under the Bodhi tree with the intention of discovering in meditation "perfect knowledge.[139] "Then," records the *Acts of the Buddha*, "he sat down on his hams in a posture, immovably firm and with his limbs gathered into a mass like a sleeping serpent's hood, exclaiming, 'I will not rise from this position on the earth until I have obtained my utmost aim.'"[140] During his meditation, he remembered his thousands of deaths and rebirths. As he relived these transmigrations, he grew in compassion "for all living beings."[141] His experience of

---

[135] Asvaghosa, book V, no. 1 (accessed June 6, 22).
[136] Asvaghosa, book XII, no. 92 (accessed June 6, 22).
[137] Asvaghosa, book XII, no. 98 (accessed June 6, 22).
[138] Asvaghosa, book XII, no. 103 (accessed June 6, 22).
[139] Asvaghosa, book XII, no. 116 (accessed June 6, 22).
[140] Asvaghosa, book XII, no. 117 (accessed June 6, 22).
[141] Asvaghosa, book XIV, no. 4 (accessed June 6, 22).

being enlightened earned him the name Buddha, which comes from the Sanskrit word *bodhati* meaning "is awake, observes, understands."[142]

After experiencing this high state of consciousness, he felt impelled to pass into nirvana and cease experiencing rebirth and death by remaining in a mentally immobile state. Instead, he choose the way of compassion and stayed on earth in order to pass on his way of life to others. When he had sufficiently taught the Middle Way of enlightenment, he died and entered into nirvana, and, according to Buddhist doctrine, was saved by being freed from suffering.[143]

According to the later Mahayana school of Buddhism, once passing into nirvana the Buddha became transformed into a cosmic body that encompasses the universe which at times intervenes in its affairs in order to assist others on the path to enlightenment.[144] Other schools, sometimes called the Old Wisdom School or Hinayana, equate nirvana with "total self-extinction."[145] The idea of the Siddhartha Buddha as a savior, consequently, is more pronounced in the Mahayana school.

In contrasting Buddhist salvation with Christian

---

[142] "Buddha," Online Etymology Dictionary, http://etymonline.com/index.php?allowed_in_frame=0&search=buddha&searchmode=none, (accessed Jun 22, 2015).

[143] Grant Hardy, *Great Minds of the Eastern Intellectual Tradition*, Lectures 1-18 (Chantilly: The Teaching Company, 2011), 48-49.

[144] Edward Conze, *Buddhism: Its Essence and Development* (New York: Dover, 2003) 188-189.

[145] Conze, 112-121, 188.

salvation, Pope St. John Paul II in *Crossing the Threshold of Hope* writes:

> The *Buddhist doctrine of salvation* constituted the central point, or rather the only point, of this system. Nevertheless, both the Buddhist tradition and the methods deriving from it have an almost exclusively *negative soteriology*.
>
> The "enlightenment" experienced by Buddha comes down to the conviction that the world is bad, that it is the source of evil and of suffering for man. To liberate oneself from this evil, one must free oneself from this world, necessitating a break with the ties that join us to external reality-ties existing in our human nature, in our psyche, in our bodies. The more we are liberated from these ties, the more we become indifferent to what is in the world, and the more we are freed from suffering, from the evil that has its source in the world.
>
> Do we draw near to God in this way? This is not mentioned in the "enlightenment" conveyed by Buddha. Buddhism is in large measure an *"atheistic" system*. We do not free ourselves from evil through the good which comes from God; we liberate ourselves only through detachment from the world, which is bad. The fullness of such a detachment is not union with God, but what is called nirvana, a state of perfect indifference with regard to the world. *To save oneself* means, above all, to free oneself from evil by becoming

indifferent to the world, *which is the source of evil.* This is the culmination of the spiritual process.¹⁴⁶

¹⁴⁷

Four Noble Truths

After his enlightenment, the Buddha, in his first post-enlightenment lesson, gave the following teaching to his disciples. In it are contained what is referred to as the Four Noble Truths. These four assertions are commonly considered, explains the *Buddhist Diction-*

---

¹⁴⁶ John Paul II, *Crossing the Threshold of Hope*, trans. Jenny McPhee and Martha McPhee (New York: Alfred A. Knopf, 2005), 85-86.

¹⁴⁷ พระมหาเทวประภาส วชิรญาณเมธี (ผู้ถ่าย-ปล่อยสัญญาอนุญาตภาพให้นำไปใช้ได้เพื่อการศึกษาโดยอยู่ภายใต้ cc-by-sa-3.0), "reaching Buddha (Dharmacakra mudrā). Gupta period. Sandstone, H. 160 cm. Archaeological Museum (ASI), Sarnath, India. Location:Sarnath Museum, India," photograph, https://commons.wikimedia.org/wiki/File%3ABuddha_in_Sarnath_Museum_(Dhammajak_Mutra).jpg, (accessed June 23, 2015).

ary, "the briefest synthesis of the entire teachings of Buddhism, since all those manifold doctrines of the threefold Canon (*Tipitaka*) are without exception, included therein. They are [1] the truth of suffering, [2] the origin of suffering, [3] the extinction of suffering, and [4] of the Eight-fold Path leading to the extinction of suffering."[148] These four can be categorized as sickness, the cause of the sickness, the cure in a general way, and the cure specified. The sickness is suffering. The cause of suffering is desire (or craving). The cure in a general way is rejecting desire. The cure when specified entails practicing the eight-fold path which includes right thinking, right acting, and right willing.

~ The Four Noble Truths ~

[1] Suffering, as a noble truth, is this: Birth is suffering, aging is suffering, sickness is suffering, death is suffering, sorrow and lamentation, pain, grief and despair are suffering; association with the loathed is suffering, dissociation from the loved is suffering, not to get what one wants is suffering — in short, suffering is the five categories of clinging objects.

[2] The origin of suffering, as a noble truth, is this: It is the craving that produces renewal of being accompanied by enjoyment and lust, and

---

[148] Nyanatiloka Thera, *Buddhist Dictionary: Manual of Buddhist Terms and Doctrines*, Fifth Revised Ed., (Kandy: Buddhist Publication Society, 2004), 165.

enjoying this and that; in other words, craving for sensual desires, craving for being, craving for non-being.

[3] Cessation of suffering, as a noble truth, is this: It is remainderless fading and ceasing, giving up, relinquishing, letting go and rejecting, of that same craving.

[4] The way leading to cessation of suffering, as a noble truth, is this: It is simply the noble eightfold path, that is to say, right view, right intention; right speech, right action, right livelihood; right effort, right mindfulness, right concentration.[149]

Eight-Fold Path

In his first post-enlightenment speech, the Buddha succinctly enumerates the means to use in striving for enlightenment and nirvana. He states, "It is the Noble Eight-fold path, and nothing else, namely: right understanding, right thought, right speech, right action, right livelihood, right effort, right mindfulness and right concentration. This is the Middle Path realized by the Tathagata [the Buddha] which gives vision, which gives knowledge, and leads

---

[149] "Dhammacakkappavattana Sutta: Setting in Motion the Wheel of Truth" (SN 56.11), translated from the Pali by Ñanamoli Thera. *Access to Insight (Legacy Edition)*, 13 June 2010, http://www.accesstoinsight.org/tipitaka/sn/sn56/sn56.011.nymo.html .

to calm, to insight, to enlightenment, and to Nibbana [Nirvana]."[150]

This eight-fold path can be broken down into the following categories.

Philosophy (or Wisdom)	Morality (or Ethics)	Spirituality
1. "Right View or Understanding"	3. "Right Speech"	6. "Right Effort"
2. "Right Thoughts or Intentions"	4. "Right Action"	7. "Right Mindfulness"
	5. " Right Livelihood"	8. "Right Concentration"[151]

Moral Precepts: Five, Eight, and Ten

Siddhartha Buddha's moderate Middle Path allowed for the development of various moral codes according to one's role. Listed below are three such training codes from a Theravada branch of Buddhism.

---

[150] "Dhammacakkappavattana Sutta: Setting in Motion the Wheel of Truth" (SN 56.11), translated from the Pali by Piyadassi Thera. *Access to Insight (Legacy Edition)*, 30 November 2013, http://www.accesstoinsight.org/tipitaka/sn/sn56/sn56.011.piya.html .

[151] The direct quotes are within quotations. The schema is mine. Venerable Dr. Balangoda Ananda Maitreya Mahanayaka Thera Abhidhaja Maharatthaguru Aggamaha Pandita DLitt D Litt, Jayasili, *Introducing Buddhism* (Taipei: The Corporate Body of the Buddha Educational Foundation, 1993), 6.

The first two are for laity. The last is for monks and nuns.

~ Five Moral Precepts for the Laity ~

1. No Arms Trading
2. No Human Trafficking
3. Avoid Meat
4. Avoid Alcohol
5. Avoid Poison[152]

~ Eight Moral Precepts for the Laity ~

1. Avoid killing living beings.
2. No stealing.
3. No sexual misconduct.
4. No lying.
5. No backbiting.
6. No harsh and angry speech.
7. No gossip.
8. No immoral employment.[153]

~ Ten Moral Precepts for Monks and Nuns ~

Practical = growth in four immeasurables and

---

[152] Not a direct quote. Nyanatiloka Thera, *Buddhist Dictionary: Manual of Buddhist Terms and Doctrines*, Fifth Revised Ed., (Kandy: Buddhist Publication Society, 2004), 204.

[153] Not a direct quote. Venerable Dr. Balangoda Ananda Maitreya Mahanayaka Thera Abhidhaja Maharatthaguru Aggamaha Pandita DLitt D Litt, Jayasili, *Introducing Buddhism* (Taipei: The Corporate Body of the Buddha Educational Foundation, 1993), 37.

Nirvana.

1. I undertake the training rule to refrain from taking life.
2. I undertake the training rule to refrain from stealing.
3. I undertake the training rule to refrain from sexual intercourse.
4. I undertake the training rule to refrain from telling lies.
5. I undertake the training rule to refrain from intoxicating fermented & distilled beverages that lead to carelessness.
6. I undertake the training rule to refrain from eating at the wrong time.
7. I undertake the training rule to refrain from dancing, singing, music, & watching shows.
8. I undertake the training rule to refrain from wearing garlands and beautifying myself with perfumes & cosmetics.
9. I undertake the training rule to refrain from high & luxurious seats & beds.
10. I undertake the training rule to refrain from accepting gold & money.[154]

---

[154] "The Khuddakapatha," (Khp 1-9), translated from the Pali by Thanissaro Bhikkhu. Access to Insight (Legacy Edition), 30 November 2013, http://www.accesstoinsight.org/tipitaka/kn/khp/khp.1-9.than.html .

Fr. Peter Samuel Kucer, MSA

Quiz 7 for Chapter 7

1-2. Why did Siddhartha Buddha consider his spiritual path a Middle Way? In answering this question name the two extremes he thought Buddhism falls between.

3-6. Describe the life of Siddhartha Gautama. Include the following: his father, beautiful women, asceticism, and enlightenment.

7-12. In *Crossing the Threshold of Hope*, how does Pope St. John Paul II contrast Buddhist teaching on salvation with Christian teaching? Include in your answer the following: negative soteriology, positive soteriology, atheism, theism, saving oneself, and grace.

13-17. State the Four Noble Truths. With respect to the Catholic understanding of salvation explain what is absent from these Four Noble Truths.

13.

14.

15.

16.

17.

18-21. How are the Ten Moral Precepts for Buddhist monks and nuns similar and different from Catholic rules for monasteries and convents? In answering, state at least two similarities and two differences. You might be interested in referring to St. Benedict's rule number forty and St. Paul Timothy:

~ St. Benedict's Rule Number 40 ~

"Everyone has his own gift from God, one in this way and another in that." It is therefore with some misgiving we regulate the measure of other men's sustenance. Nevertheless, keeping in view the needs of weaker brethren, we believe that a hemina of wine a day is sufficient for each…[155]

~ St. Paul's First Letter to Timothy 5:23 ~

No longer drink only water, but take a little wine for the sake of your stomach and your frequent ailments. (NRSV)

---

[155] St. Benedict, *St. Benedict's Rule for Monasteries*, trans. Leonard J. Doyle (Collegeville: The Liturgical Press, 1948), 58.

Chapter 8: Mahayana, Theravada and Tibetan Buddhism

Introduction

In the previous chapter, you may have noticed that the same Buddhist term is spelled, and pronounced, in two distinct manners. For example, the state that the Buddha entered after his enlightenment or awakening is spelled both *nirvana* and *nibbana*. The two different ways of spelling the same term are similar since they come from two dialects of Sanskrit, the ancient language of India. Etymologically *nirvana/nibbana* means "a blowing out".[156] In Latin, this term translates as *de-spiration*,[157] which is never a goal in Christianity since Christians aim at being inspired and filled with the Spirit of God, not blown out. The second spelling is a dialect of Sanskrit

---

[156] "Nirvana," Online Etymology Dictionary http://etymonline.com/index.php?allowed_in_frame=0&search=nirvana&searchmode=none, (accessed July 5, 2015).

[157] "Nirvana," Online Etymology Dictionary.

called Pali. Pali is used in early Buddhist writings. It is also the liturgical language of the Theravada school of Buddhism. Since this school is not the predominant school of Buddhism, the term *nirvana* is more frequently used.[158]

The most common form of Buddhism is Mahayana Buddhism. It is followed by Theravada Buddhism, which is in turn followed by Tibetan Buddhism, also called Vajrayana Buddhism. Mahayana Buddhism, predominates in China, Japan, South Korea, and Vietnam. Theravada Buddhism is mainly present in Thailand, Burma, Sri Lanka, Laos, and Cambodia. Tibetan Buddhism is primarily in in Tibet, Nepal, Bhutan, and Mongolia. In 2010, the total number of Buddhists in the world, according to Pew Research, was around 488 million.[159] The map below is based on Pew Research data. As is evident, the vast majority of Buddhists are located in Asia.

---

[158] John Snelling, *The Buddhist Handbook: A Complete Guide to Buddhist Schools, Teaching, Practice, and History* (Rochester: Inner Traditions International, 1998), 81.

[159] "Buddhist: The Global Religious Landscape," The Pew Research Center, http://www.pewforum.org/2012/12/18/global-religious-landscape-buddhist/ (accessed July 5, 2015).

Eastern Civilization from a Catholic Viewpoint

[160] TheGreenEditor, Own work, data from Pew Research Center Global Religious Landscape 2010 and

Origin of Buddhist Traditions

After Siddhartha Buddha died in c. 480 BC, disputes arose over various aspects that the Buddha deliberately left ambiguous. Councils were convened to settle these disputes. The first was held c. 405 BC. The second council was held c. 305 BC.[161]

Of these two councils, we have more reliable documentation from the second. At the Second Buddhist Council, or sometime after, a division occurred in Buddhism that some call a great schism.[162] The two main rival groups that were formed as a result of this division were called the *Sthaviravada* (Doctrine of the Elders) and the *Mahasamghtka* (Great Community). The two major schools of Buddhism that exist today are successors of these two schools. The *Theravada* school, primarily in South East Asia, is the successor of the *Sthaviravada* school. The *Mahayana* school, primarily in North Asia, East Asia, and Vietnam, is *Mahasamghtka's* successor. Sixteen other schools also arose, but none of these has survived intact.[163]

---

most recent census reports, "Map of the distribution of Buddhists in the world," map, https://commons.wikimedia.org/wiki/File%3ABuddhist_distribution.png, (accessed July 5, 2015).

[161] Damien Keown, and Charles S. Prebish, *Encyclopedia of Buddhism* (New York: Routledge, 2010), xv.

[162] Bibhuti Baruah, *Buddhist Sects and Sectarianism* (New Delhi: Sarup & Sons, 2000), 38.

[163] Malcolm David Eckel, *Great World Religions: Buddhism*, Course Guidebook (Chantilly: The Teaching Company, 2003), 24-25.

The unclear nature of Buddhist doctrine which gave rise to these divisions was intended by Siddhartha Buddha, as an account from his life in the *Sutta Pittaka* illustrates. According to this story, one of his disciples, by the name of Malunkyaputta, approached the Buddha to ask him doctrinal questions, including whether the universe is eternal, whether the soul and body are the same, and whether after death a Buddha exists.

The Buddha dismissed Malunkyaputta's questioning by comparing it to a man who has been wounded by a poisonous arrow but refuses to allow a surgeon to remove the arrow until he knows who shot him, what he looked like, what the shaft is made of, etc. With this comparison, the Buddha taught Malunkyaputta not to focus on doctrinal questions but rather to accept the practical solution to suffering that the Buddha had offered to him. If he followed the Buddha's teaching on faith, then his arrow of suffering would be removed.[164]

Catholics believe that doctrine does matter and helps to accurately know God so as to better love, glorify, and serve Him. As the *Catechism of the Catholic Church* clearly states, "Admittedly, in speaking about God like this, our language is using human modes of expression; nevertheless, it really

---

[164] "Cula-Malunkyovada Sutta: The Shorter Instructions to Malunkya" (MN 63), translated from the Pali by Thanissaro Bhikkhu. *Access to Insight (Legacy Edition)*, 30 November 2013, http://www.accesstoinsight.org/tipitaka/mn/mn.063.than.html (accessed July 7, 2015).

does attain to God himself, though unable to express him in his infinite simplicity."[165]

Theravada Buddhism

According to the system of *Theravada* (Way of the Elders) Buddhism, the Buddha only provided a good example to follow in order to be freed from suffering, extinguish desire, be awakened, and to enter into the state of *Nibbana* (Pali for the Sanskrit term *Nirvana*). The awakening from this world of illusion can only be obtained by monks and nuns who live out celibacy and commit themselves to a life of intensive study and meditation.[166] Once the Buddha enters the state of Nibbana, he cannot be communicated with. This means that prayers to a spiritually awakened person are without purpose.[167]

An enlightened person cannot communicate with the world or the world communicate with it since the person has realized the Buddhist doctrine of no-self called *anatta*. This doctrine maintains that nothing has any permanent nature, identity, I, or self. As recorded by Steven Collins, the highly respected and

---

[165] *Catechism of the Catholic Church*, (Liguori: Liguori Publications, 1994), no. 43, 17.

[166] Grant Hardy, *Great Minds of the Eastern Intellectual Tradition* (Chantilly: The Teaching Company, 2011), 191.

[167] Bibhuti Baruah, *Buddhist Sects and Sectarianism* (New Delhi: Sarup & Sons, 2000), 209; Steven Collins, *Selfless Persons: Imagery and Thought in Theravada Buddhism* (Cambridge: Cambridge University Press, 1982), 16.

well-educated Theravada Buddhist monk Rahula explains the doctrine of *anatta* as follows:

> What in general is suggested by Soul, Self, Ego, or to use the Sanskrit expression *Atman*, is that in man there is a permanent, everlasting and absolute entity, which is the unchanging substance behind the changing phenomenal world. According to some religions, each individual has such a separate soul which is created by God, and which, finally after death, lives eternally either in hell or heaven, its destiny depending on the judgment of its creator. According to others, it goes through many lives till it is completely purified and becomes finally united with God or *Brahman*, Universal Soul or *Atman*, from which it originally emanated. This soul or self in man is the thinker of thoughts, feeler of sensations, and receiver of rewards and punishments for all its actions good or bad. Such a conception is called the idea of self.
>
> Buddhism stands unique in the history of human thought in denying the existence of such a Soul, Self, or *Atman*. According to the teaching of the Buddha, the idea of self is an imaginary, false belief which has no corresponding reality, and it produces harmful thoughts of 'me' and 'mine', selfish desire, craving, attachment, hatred, ill-will, conceit, pride, egotism, and other defilements, impurities and problems. It is the source of all the troubles in the world from personal conflicts to wars between nations. In short, to this false view

can be traced all the evil in the world.[168]

The radical insistence that nothing has any enduring self raises the question of whether the doctrine of *anatta* contradicts the doctrine of reincarnation, for in order for something to be reincarnated there must be some type of continuity from one existence to the next. As Malcolm David Eckel pithily asks, "If there is no self, what is reborn?"[169] The Theravada school's response is, explains Eckel, "The 'stream' or 'flame' of consciousness (*vi-ana*) [is reborn]. Because of the causal continuity between moments in the flame, it is possible to say that I am the 'same' person from one moment to the next."[170] In other words, while denying, with the doctrine of *anatta*, that there is any permanent self, the Theravada schools at the same time affirm that there is a personality that is defined by the causal relationship of one moment to the next.

The Catholic position, teaches the *Catechism of the Catholic Church*, is "that every spiritual soul is created immediately by God – it is not 'produced' by the parents – and also that it is immortal: it does not perish when it separates from the body at death, and it will be reunited with the body at the final Resurrec-

---

[168] Steven Collins, *Selfless Persons: Imagery and Thought in Theravada Buddhism* (Cambridge: Cambridge University Press, 1982), 4.

[169] Eckel, 14.

[170] Eckel, 14.

tion."[171]

Monks Taking an Exam in Myanmar, a Predominantly Theravada Buddhist Country[172]

Mahayana Buddhism

As explained earlier, the Mahayana school of Buddhism developed out of the earlier *Mahāsāṃghika* school, which means Great Community. Mahayana means Great Vehicle. As the Great Vehicle, Mahayana deems other Buddhist schools, including Theravada, as lesser vehicles, which is what the

---

[171] *Catechism of the Catholic Church*, (Liguori: Liguori Publications, 1994), no. 366, 93.

[172] magical-world, "Monk examinations, Bago, Myanmar," photograph, https://upload.wikimedia.org/wikipedia/commons/6/6d/Monk_examinations%2C_Bago%2C_Myanmar.jpg, (accessed July 6, 2015).

somewhat derogatory term Hinayana Buddhism means.[173] The only school that has lasted among these supposedly lesser vehicle schools is Theravada. Hence, Theravada is often called Hinayana Buddhism.

One major distinguishing feature between Mahayana and Theravada concerns the doctrine of no-self (*anatta* in Pali and *anatman* in Sanskrit). As explained by Eckel, "The Mahayana takes the concept of no-self a step further. It denies the reality of a permanent self and the reality of the momentary phenomena that make up the flow of the personality. This Mahayana position is expressed by saying that everything that is 'empty' (*shunya*) of identity (*svabhava* or *atman*). The nature of all things is simply their 'Emptiness' (*shunyata*)."[174] Mahayana, therefore, has greater difficulty in answering the question of, "If there is no self, what is reborn?"[175] The Buddhist Indian Mahayana philosopher Nagarjuna (c. 150-250 AD) explains the Mahayana doctrine of emptiness as follows:[176]

~ Nagarjuna on Emptiness ~

18. Whatever is dependently co-arisen
That is explained to be emptiness.
That, being a dependent designation,
Is itself the middle way.

---

[173] Eckel, 26.
[174] Eckel, 33.
[175] Eckel, 14.
[176] Nagarjuna is also a founder of a Mahayana school of Buddhism.

19. Something that is not dependently arisen,
Such a thing does not exist.
Therefore a non-empty thing
Does not exist.[177]

Nagarjuna's radical doctrine of emptiness means that if there is no self, even in a momentary causal manner in a stream of reality, then ultimately all differences are but an illusion, including the difference between good or evil, male or female, nirvana and samsara, Buddha and the un-awakened. Catholicism, in contrast, asserts that difference does actually exist. The world is different from God but not in a way that God plus the world is greater than God prior to the creation of the world. This is because the created world only has existence, has being, since it participates, without being equal to, God who is being.

A Buddhist school that followed these assertions to their logical conclusions is the Tantric school. The Tantric School held that "the wise man renders himself free of impurity by means of impurity itself."[178] Some Tantric followers interpret this radical non-dualism, which entails even sexual difference is

---

[177] Nagarjuna, *The Fundamental Wisdom of the Middle Way: Nagarjuna's Mulamadhyamakakaarika*, trans. Jay L. Garfield (Oxford: Oxford University Press, 1995), Chapter XXIV, "Examination of the Four Noble Truths", nos. 19-19, 69.

[178] Eckel, 35. Eckel cites from the Tantric text *Cittavisuddhiprakarana* in *Buddhist Texts through the Ages*, trans. David Snellgrove, (New York: Harper & Row, 1964), 221.

but an illusion, by ritually copulating during meditation as a way of denying difference. This ritual is performed in order represent in bodily form the Tantric belief that there is no-difference between anything.[179] Statues of the Buddha having intercourse with a woman also represent the Tantric belief of radical no-difference and non-duality.

A principle lesson of these sexual depictions of the Buddha is that ultimately there is nothing to possess or desire since, as the doctrine of non-duality teaches, the object of our desire is an illusion. This is counter to the thought of Benedict XVI on *eros* and *agape* that was discussed in a previous chapter. Catholicism teaches that desirous love exists since there is actual differences in the world with some similarity. This is particularly true in the relationship between human beings and God. God is the ultimate different Thou that we desire to possess, and our hearts are restless, as St. Augustine (354-430 AD) teaches in his *Confession*, until our desires rest in the obtaining Him.

To further bring to the fore their radical non-dualism, Tantra Buddhists created statues of the Buddha that instead of looking serene appear filled with wrath and/or passion.[180]

---

[179] Eckel, 35.
[180] Eckel, 35.

Eastern Civilization from a Catholic Viewpoint

Wrathful Deities *bodhisattvas*

Hevajra[181]

---

[181] User:Miuki, "Hevajra, wrathful emanation of the water element, important in the tantric practices of the sakya school of tibetan buddhism," photograph, https://commons.wikimedia.org/wiki/File:Hevajra.jpg, (accessed July 7, 2015).

Yamantaka[182]

Pictured above are two Tantric *bodhisattvas*, or gods. Mahayana and Tantric Buddhism affirms the existence of Gods but never of a creating God as monotheism does. The Mahayana understanding of bodhisattva gods reveals a second significant dif-

---

[182] Online Collection of Brooklyn Museum; Photo: Brooklyn Museum, 69.164.9.jpg, "Vajrabhairava Yamantaka," photograph, https://commons.wikimedia.org/wiki/File%3ABrooklyn_Museum_-_Vajrabhairava_Yamantaka_-_Anonymous.jpg, (accessed July 7, 2015).

ference between the Mahayana and the Theravada Buddhist traditions.

According to Mahayana Buddhism, a person who is about to obtain nirvana but then out of compassions chooses not to is called a bodhisattva, in Sanskrit literally "enlightenment being." This term bears with it the additional meaning of a "being (*Sattva*) intent on achieving enlightenment (*Bodhi*)."[183] As explained by Eckel, "a bodhisattva aspires to achieve Buddhahood for the sake of all other beings. Eventually, even bodhisattvas become Buddhas when their aspirations have reached fruition and their practice of the path is complete."[184]

The following chart identifies the eight great celestial bodhisattvas to whom Mahayana Buddhists practice devotions out of a belief that these compassionate, heavenly beings will lead them to being awakened and freed from suffering. Devotion to the bodhisattvas arose at the same time as Indians began increasing their worship of Hindu Gods. Some scholars maintain that Mahayana Buddhist bodhisattva doctrine was at least partially due to devotion to Hindu Gods.[185]

---

[183] Robert E. Buswell, and Donald S. Lopez, *The Princeton Dictionary of Buddhism* (Princeton: Princeton University Press, 2014), 134.

[184] Eckel, 27.

[185] Leslie Kawamura, *Bodhisattva Doctrine in Buddhism* (Waterloo: Wilfrid Laurier University Press, 1981), 45-46.

Eight Bodhisattvas[186]	Perfection and Ability Associated with the Bodhisattvas
Manjushri	Wisdom
Avalokiteshvara	Compassion
Vajrapani	Power
Maitreya	Love
Kshitigarbha	Fruitfulness of the Land
Akashagarbha	Purifying Transgressions
Sarvanivaranavishkambhin	Purifying Obstructions
Samantabhadra	Intercessory Prayer

The second mentioned difference between Theravada Buddhism and Mahayana Buddhism is seen with great clarity within the Mahayana school of Buddhism called Pure Land. Pure Land Buddhism further developed the Mahayana belief in bodhisattvas who, out of the compassionate desire to "attain enlightenment for the sake of all other sentient beings,"[187] deny themselves nirvana in order to help others on the path to nirvana. This Mahayana understanding of bodhisattvas bears with it the concept of relying on others and not on self to escape suffering and be awakened. Since salvation from suffering can

---

[186] "Eight great bodhisattvas," Rigpa Shedra, http://www.rigpawiki.org/index.php?title=Eight_great_bodhisattvas, (accessed July 7, 2015).

[187] A common aspiratory prayer in Mahayana Buddhism is "May I attain enlightenment for the sake of all other sentient beings." "How of (The Buddhas)," http://chakrasamvaracenter.com/, Chakra Samvara Center, (accessed July 8, 2015).

be obtained by relying on the perfections of others, Mahayana also teaches that all are to aspire to be bodhisattvas and to Buddha-hood.

In contrast, Theravada Buddhists, while also referring to bodhisattvas in their tradition, do not hold up bodhisattvas or Buddha-hood as the ideal for all to aspire. This explains why Theravada Buddhism did not develop the bodhisattva doctrine as much as the Mahayana did. In Theravada Buddhism, there is such high esteem given to the bodhisattvas and Buddha-hood that it is held out as an ideal for a select, exceptional few and not for all.[188]

The practical effect of these two different traditions on the role of the bodhisattva is evident in two different ways of understanding dependency and brings out a third difference between Theravada Buddhism and Mahayana Buddhism. In Theravada Buddhism, self-dependency is stressed more. In Mahayana Buddhism, dependence on others is brought to the fore, particularly in Pure Land Buddhism.[189]

Pure Land Buddhism promotes reliance on others in order to obtain nirvana with its devotion to Amitabha Buddha. According to a Mahayana story when Amitabha was but a bodhisattva he promised that when he obtained Buddha-hood he would create

---

[188] Karel Werner, Jeffrey Samuels, Bhikkhu Bodhi, Peter Skilling, Bhikkhu Anālayo, and David McMahan, *The Bodhisattva Ideal: Essays on the Emergence of Mahayana* (Kandy: Buddhist Publication Society, 2013), 42-43.

[189] Eckel, 32.

a highly pleasurable place into which all could be reborn as long as they relied on him. All that is required is to remember his name in an undistracted manner.[190]

~ The Pure Land Promised by Amitabha ~

2. Then the Buddha addressed Shariputra, the elder, and said, 'Beyond a hundred thousand kotis of Buddha-lands westwards from here, there is a world named Sukhavati. In that world there is a Buddha, Amita(-ayus) by name, now dwelling and preaching the law. Shariputra, why is that country named Sukhavati? The living beings in that country have no pains, but receive pleasures only. Therefore, it is called Sukhavati.

....

7. 'Shariputra, what do you think in your mind, for what reason that Buddha is called Amita(-abha)? Shariputra, the light of that Buddha is boundless and shining without impediments all over the countries of the ten quarters. Therefore he is called Amita(-abha). Again, Shariputra, the life of that Buddha and of his people is endless and boundless in Asamkhya-kalpas, so he is

---

[190] Eckel, 30.

named Amita(-ayus). Shariputra, since Buddha Amitayus attained Buddhahood, (it has passed) now ten Kalpas. Again, Shariputra, that Buddha has numerous Shravakas or disciples, who are all Arhats and whose number cannot be known by (ordinary) calculation. (The number of) Bodhisattvas (cannot be known) also. Shariputra, that Buddha-land is arrayed with such good qualities and adornments.

8. 'Again, Shariputra, the beings born in the land Sukhavati are all Avinivartaniya. Among them is a multitude of beings bound to one birth only; and their number, being extremely large, cannot be expressed by (ordinary) calculation. Only can it be mentioned in boundless Asamkhya-kalpas. Shariputra, the sentient beings who hear (this account) ought to put up their prayer that they may be born into that country; for they will be able to be in the same place together with those noble personages. Shariputra, by means of small good works [lit. roots] or virtues no one can be born in that country.

9. 'Shariputra, if there be a good man or a good woman, who, on hearing of Buddha Amitayus, keeps his name (in

mind) with thoughts undisturbed for one day, two days, three days, four days, five days, six days, or seven days, that person, when about to die, (will see) Amitayus Buddha accompanied by his holy host appear before him; and immediately after his death, he with his mind undisturbed can be born into the Sukhavati land of Buddha Amitayus. Shariputra, as I witness this benefit, I say these words; every being who listens to this preaching ought to offer up prayer with the desire to be born into that country.

...

16. 'Shariputra, what do you think in your mind, why it is called the Sutra approved and protected by all the Buddhas? Shariputra, if there be a good man or a good woman who listens to those Buddhas' invocation of the name (of Buddha Amitayus) and the name of this Sutra, that good man or woman will be protected by all the Buddhas and never fail to attain Anuttara-samyak-sambodhi. For this reason, Shariputra, all of you should believe in my words and in what all the Buddhas proclaim. Shariputra, if there are men who have already made, are now making, or shall make, prayer with the desire to be born in the land of Buddha Amitayus, they

never fail to attain Anuttara-samyaksambodhi, and have been born, are now being born, or shall be born in that country. Therefore, Shariputra, a good man or good woman who has the faith ought to offer up prayers to be born in that land.

17. 'Shariputra, as I am now praising the inconceivable excellences of those Buddhas, so all those Buddhas are magnifying the inconceivable excellences of myself, saying these words: Shakyamuni, the Buddha, has successfully achieved a rare thing of extreme difficulty; he has attained Anuttara-samyaksambodhi in the Saha world in the evil period of five corruptions -- Corruption of Kalpa, Corruption of Belief, Corruption of Passions, Corruption of Living Beings, and Corruption of Life; and for the sake of all the sentient beings he is preaching the Law which is not easy to accept. Shariputra, you must see that in the midst of this evil world of five corruptions I have achieved this difficult thing of attaining Anuttara-samyak-sambodhi, and for the benefit of all the beings I am preaching the Law which is difficult to be accepted. This is how it is esteemed as (a thing of) extreme diffi-

culty.'

> The Buddha having preached this Sutra, Shariputra and Bhikshus, and Devas, men, Asuras, etc., of all the worlds, who have listened to the Buddha's preaching, believed and accepted with joy, made worship, and went away.[191]

Tibetan Buddhism

Tibetan Buddhism is named after the land that is situated northeast of India and which borders China. This form of Buddhism is well-known in the West, mainly because of the immigration of many Tibetans to Western lands in order to be freed of political repression by the government of China. Tibetan Buddhism is a synthesis of Theravada, Mahayana, and Tantric Buddhism.[192]

A distinguishing feature of one form of Tibetan Buddhism, called the Yellow Hats or Virtuous Way, is

---

[191] "The Smaller Sutra on Amida Buddha Amidakyo, or The Smaller Sukhavativyuha Sutra," trans. from the Chinese Version of Kumarajiva by Nishu Utsuki, True Shin Buddhism, http://web.mit.edu/stclair/www/smaller.html, (accessed July 8, 2015). According to the website, the quoted text is public domain. "This electronic version may be copied and distributed free and without permission provided that it is not altered in any way."

[192] Dalai Lama, "Reincarnation," DalaiLama.com, http://dalailama.com/messages/statement-of-his-holiness-the-fourteenth-dalai-lama-tenzin-gyatso-on-the-issue-of-his-reincarnation, (accessed July 8, 2015).

the belief that their political and spiritual leader, the Dalai Lama, is a reincarnation of the previous Dalai Lama who in turn is a reincarnation of the preceding one and so forth. The current Dalai Lama of the Virtuous Way Buddhism is believed to have been reincarnated fourteen times. Since 1959, the fourteenth Dalai Lama has been living in exile from his homeland.[193]

The current Dalai Lama has offered to be the last of the Dalai Lamas. In explaining this possibility, he stated:

...

In the course of upholding the Buddhist tradition in Tibet, we evolved a unique Tibetan tradition of recognizing the reincarnations of scholar-adepts that has been of immense help to both the Dharma and sentient beings, particularly to the monastic community.

...

The Dalai Lamas have functioned as both the political and spiritual leaders of Tibet for 369 years since 1642. I have now voluntarily brought this to an end, proud and satisfied that we can pursue the kind of democratic system of government flourishing elsewhere in the world. In fact, as far back as 1969, I made clear that concerned people should decide whether the Dalai Lama's reincarnations should continue in the future. However, in the absence of clear guidelines, should the concerned public express a strong wish

---

[193] Eckel, 43-47; Dalai Lama, "Reincarnation."

for the Dalai Lamas to continue, there is an obvious risk of vested political interests misusing the reincarnation system to fulfil their own political agenda. Therefore, while I remain physically and mentally fit, it seems important to me that we draw up clear guidelines to recognize the next Dalai Lama, so that there is no room for doubt or deception. For these guidelines to be fully comprehensible, it is essential to understand the system of Tulku recognition and the basic concepts behind it. Therefore, I shall briefly explain them below."

As I mentioned earlier, reincarnation is a phenomenon which should take place either through the voluntary choice of the concerned person or at least on the strength of his or her karma, merit, and prayers. Therefore, the person who reincarnates has sole legitimate authority over where and how he or she takes rebirth and how that reincarnation is to be recognized. It is a reality that no one else can force the person concerned, or manipulate him or her. It is particularly inappropriate for Chinese communists, who explicitly reject even the idea of past and future lives, let alone the concept of reincarnate Tulkus, to meddle in the system of reincarnation and especially the reincarnations of the Dalai Lamas and Panchen Lamas. Such brazen meddling contradicts their own political ideology and reveals their double standards. Should this situation continue in the future, it will be impossible for Tibetans and those who follow the Tibetan Buddhist tradition to acknowledge or accept it.

When I am about ninety I will consult the high Lamas of the Tibetan Buddhist traditions, the Tibetan public, and other concerned people who follow Tibetan Buddhism, and re-evaluate whether the institution of the Dalai Lama should continue or not. On that basis we will take a decision. If it is decided that the reincarnation of the Dalai Lama should continue and there is a need for the Fifteenth Dalai Lama to be recognized, responsibility for doing so will primarily rest on the concerned officers of the Dalai Lama's Gaden Phodrang Trust. They should consult the various heads of the Tibetan Buddhist traditions and the reliable oath-bound Dharma Protectors who are linked inseparably to the lineage of the Dalai Lamas. They should seek advice and direction from these concerned beings and carry out the procedures of search and recognition in accordance with past tradition. I shall leave clear written instructions about this. Bear in mind that, apart from the reincarnation recognized through such legitimate methods, no recognition or acceptance should be given to a candidate chosen for political ends by anyone, including those in the People's Republic of China.[194]

---

[194] Dalai Lama, "Reincarnation."

Quiz 8 for Chapter 8

1-5. Discuss the Buddhist concept of Nirvana in relationship to the Catholic doctrine of sanctification. Include in your response the following: definition of the term nirvana, translation of nirvana in Latin, the Holy Spirit, and human nature.

6-8. Place the following in the corresponding categories: Mahayana Buddhism, Theravada Buddhism, and Tibetan Buddhism.

6.	Nepal, Bhutan and Mongolia
7.	Thailand, Burma, Sri Lanka, Laos and Cambodia
8.	China, Japan, South Korea and Vietnam.

9-11. Why did disputes arise in Buddhism soon after Siddhartha Buddha died? In answering this question include the following: theory (or doctrine), and practice. Also, how do you think the role of doctrine differs in Catholicism from the role of doctrine as held by Siddhartha Buddha?

12-14. Distinguish in three ways, as explained in the chapter, Theravada Buddhism from Mahayana Buddhism.

12

13.

14.

15. Does the Mahayana teaching on emptiness contradict the teaching on reincarnation? Explain your answer.

16. Based on your reading of excerpts from the Dalai Lama's discussion on reincarnation, why does the Chinese government want to either eliminate the Dalai Lama's position or to at least control it?

134

Chapter 9: Laozi, Daoism and Chinese Buddhism

Introduction

When Mahayana Buddhists entered China they were pleased to encounter Daoism, a Chinese philosophy that is highly compatible with Buddhism. In this chapter we will first study Daoism apart from Buddhism before seeing how it resembles Buddhism, is different from Buddhism, and in some ways transformed Buddhism. A Chinese Buddhist school that represents the synthesis of Buddhism and Daoism is Chan Buddhism also called Zen Buddhism in Japan.

Daoism

The central person for Daoist ideas is the Chinese man Laozi (c. 500 BC). It is believed he lived around the time of the famous Chinese philosopher Confucius, whom we will study later. The major work attributed to Laozi is the *Daodejing*. This poetic work is interwoven with a number of central ideas including, giving prominence to attributes considered feminine, harmony among people and with nature, non-intervention, the personal, and emptiness.[195] While reading the excerpts below try to determine how these Daoist attributes are present.

~ The *Daodejing* and the Feminine ~

The valley spirit dies not, aye the same;
   The female mystery thus do we name.
   Its gate, from which at first they issued forth,
   Is called the root from which grew heaven and earth.
   Long and unbroken does its power remain,
   Used gently, and without the touch of pain.[196]

Who knows his manhood's strength,
   Yet still his female feebleness maintains;
   As to one channel flow the many drains,
   All come to him, yea, all beneath the sky.
   Thus he the constant excellence retains;
   The simple child again, free from all stains.

Who knows how white attracts,
   Yet always keeps himself within black's shade,
   The pattern of humility displayed,

---

[195] Grant Hardy, *Great Minds of the Eastern Intellectual Tradition*, Lectures 1-18 (Chantilly: The Great Courses, 2011), 90-101; Eckel, 50-51.

[196] Lao-Tse, "The Tao Teh King or The Tao and its Characteristics," part I, chap. 6, trans. James Legge, Project Gutenberg, http://www.gutenberg.org/files/216/216-h/216-h.htm, (accessed July 9, 2015).

Displayed in view of all beneath the sky;
He in the unchanging excellence arrayed,
Endless return to man's first state has made.[197]

...

There is nothing in the world more soft and weak than water, and yet for attacking things that are firm and strong there is nothing that can take precedence of it;—for there is nothing (so effectual) for which it can be changed.

[T]he female always overcomes the male by her stillness. Stillness may be considered (a sort of) abasement.[198]

...

1. Man at his birth is supple and weak; at his death, firm and strong. (So it is with) all things. Trees and plants, in their early growth, are soft and brittle; at their death, dry and withered.

2. Thus it is that firmness and strength are the concomitants of death; softness and weakness, the concomitants of life.

3. Hence he who (relies on) the strength of his forces does not conquer; and a tree which is strong will fill the out-stretched arms, (and thereby invites the feller.)

---

[197] Lao-Tse, "The Tao Teh King or The Tao and its Characteristics," part I, chap. 28, 1.

[198] Lao-Tse, "The Tao Teh King or The Tao and its Characteristics," part II, chap. 61, 2.

4. Therefore the place of what is firm and strong is below, and that of what is soft and weak is above.[199]

2. Everyone in the world knows that the soft overcomes the hard, and the weak the strong, but no one is able to carry it out in practice.[200]

In the above excerpts, attributes considered feminine are praised and exalted above masculine characteristics. According to the *Daodejing*, the following are feminine qualities: mysterious, gentle, feeble, weak, soft, still, and life giving. The feminine is also described as like a valley, like a root, the origin of a child, and like water.

~ The *Daodejing* and Harmony ~

So it is that existence and non-existence give birth the one to (the idea of) the other; that difficulty and ease produce the one (the idea of) the other; that length and shortness fashion out the one the figure of the other; that (the ideas of) height and lowness arise from the contrast of the one with the other; that the musical notes and tones become harmonious through the relation of one with another; and that being before and behind give the

---

[199] Lao-Tse, "The Tao Teh King or The Tao and its Characteristics," part II, chap. 76, 1-4.
[200] Lao-Tse, "The Tao Teh King or The Tao and its Characteristics," part II, chap. 78, 1-2.

idea of one following another.[201]

...

> Therefore the sage manages affairs without doing anything
>
> To him by whom this harmony is known,
> (The secret of) the unchanging (Tao [Dao]) is shown,
> And in the knowledge wisdom finds its throne.
> All life-increasing arts to evil turn;
> Where the mind makes the vital breath to burn,
> (False) is the strength, (and o'er it we should mourn.) [202]

An ancient Chinese symbol dating to the 1300s BC is the yin yang symbol given below. The earliest examples of this symbol are found in the oracle bones, referred to in an earlier chapter. According to the oracle bones, yang stands for sunlight or the day, and yin represents darkness or night. In time, yin and yang were defined in reference to a third reality, *qi*. In Chinese philosophy *qi* is the tension or energy caused by the yin (feminine) and yang (masculine) relationship. According to one translation of the *Daodejing*, "All beings support *yin* and embrace *yang* and the interplay of these two forces fills the universe. Yet

---

[201] Lao-Tse, "The Tao Teh King or The Tao and its Characteristics," part I, chap. 2, 2.

[202] Lao-Tse, "The Tao Teh King or The Tao and its Characteristics," part II, chap. 53, 3.

only at the still-point, between the breathing in and the breathing out, can one capture these two in perfect harmony."[203] The interplay is *qi*. *Qi* will be out of harmony if the balance between yin and yang is not maintained.[204]

[205]

---

[203] Laozi, *Tao Te Ching: The New Translation from the Tao Te Ching: The Definitive Edition*, trans. Jonathan Star (New York: Penguin, 2001), verse 42, p. 56.

[204] Robin R. Wang, "Yinyang (Yin-yang)," Internet Encyclopedia of Philosophy, http://www.iep.utm.edu/yinyang/, (accessed July 9, 2015).

[205] Klem, "English: The Yin and Yang with white representing Yang and black representing Yin. The symbol is a visual depiction of the intertwined duality of all things in nature, a common theme in Taoism. It is believed to be derived from the 14th century Tiandi Zhiran Hetu (Heaven and Earth's Natural Diagram of the River), Hetu (Diagram of River), Luoshu (Chart of Luo), Xiantian tu (Diagram of Preceding Heaven) and Taijitu (太極圖) (Diagram of the Ultimate Power). Here the diagram is shown against a feather edged grey background to ensure clarity when displayed over black or white.," diagram, https://commons.wikimedia.org/wiki/File%3AYin_and_Yang.svg, (accessed July 9, 2015).

~ The *Daodejing* and Non-Intervention ~

> The government that seems the most unwise,
> Oft goodness to the people best supplies;
> That which is meddling, touching everything,
> Will work but ill, and disappointment bring.[206]

Daoism, as represented in the *Daodejing*, opposes a strong centralized government that controls a vast amount of territory. Instead, a non-centralized, fairly weak governing structure that allows for the existence of many relatively autonomous farming-based communities is encouraged, as is evident in the following selection. Since small communities that are less developed, like the Amish, require members to rely upon one another, the Daoist emphasis is on spontaneity and individualism instead of collectivism and uniformity. This spontaneity and individualism, though, is to be shaped by a small town's personal atmosphere of intimacy.

~ The *Daodejing* and the Personal ~

80. 1. In a little state with a small population, I would so order it, that, though there were individuals with the abilities of ten or a hundred men, there should be no employment of them; I would make the people, while looking on death

---

[206] Lao-Tse, "The Tao Teh King or The Tao and its Characteristics," part II, chap. 58, 1.

as a grievous thing, yet not remove elsewhere (to avoid it).
2. Though they had boats and carriages, they should have no occasion to ride in them; though they had buff coats and sharp weapons, they should have no occasion to don or use them.
3. I would make the people return to the use of knotted cords (instead of the written characters).
4. They should think their (coarse) food sweet; their (plain) clothes beautiful; their (poor) dwellings places of rest; and their common (simple) ways sources of enjoyment.
5. There should be a neighboring state within sight, and the voices of the fowls and dogs should be heard all the way from it to us, but I would make the people to old age, even to death, not have any intercourse with it.[207]

~ The Dao (or Tao) and Emptiness ~

Ch. 1. 1. The Tao [Dao] that can be trodden is not the enduring and unchanging Tao [Dao]. The name that can be named is not the enduring and unchanging name.

---

[207] Lao-Tse, "The Tao Teh King or The Tao and its Characteristics," part II, chap. 80, 1-5.

2. (Conceived of as) having no name, it is the Originator of heaven and earth; (conceived of as) having a name, it is the Mother of all things.

3. Always without desire we must be found,
If its deep mystery we would sound;
But if desire always within us be,
Its outer fringe is all that we shall see.

4. Under these two aspects, it is really the same; but as development takes place, it receives the different names. Together we call them the Mystery. Where the Mystery is the deepest is the gate of all that is subtle and wonderful.

...

2. So it is that existence and non-existence give birth the one to (the idea of) the other; that difficulty and ease produce the one (the idea of) the other; that length and shortness fashion out the one the figure of the other; that (the ideas of) height and lowness arise from the contrast of the one with the other; that the musical notes and tones become harmonious through the relation of one with another; and that being before and behind give the idea of one following another.

3. Therefore the sage manages affairs

without doing anything, and conveys his instructions without the use of speech.

...

3. 1. Not to value and employ men of superior ability is the way to keep the people from rivalry among themselves; not to prize articles which are difficult to procure is the way to keep them from becoming thieves; not to show them what is likely to excite their desires is the way to keep their minds from disorder.

2. Therefore the sage, in the exercise of his government, empties their minds, fills their bellies, weakens their wills, and strengthens their bones.

3. He constantly (tries to) keep them without knowledge and without desire, and where there are those who have knowledge, to keep them from presuming to act (on it). When there is this abstinence from action, good order is universal.

4. 1. The Tao [Dao] is (like) the emptiness of a vessel; and in our employment of it we must be on our guard against all fullness. How deep and unfathomable it is, as if it were the Honored Ancestor of

all things![208]

Chan Buddhism

The last mentioned feature of Daoism, emptiness and inaction as more fundamental than substance and action, particularly drew the attention of Buddhists as they spread Buddhism into China during the T'ang Dynasty (618-907 AD). As practice of Buddhism increased in China, it steadily decreased in India from the 600s AD onward. At the turn of the century (1000 AD), it was practically non-existent in its native land of India. A reason for its decline, but not sole reason nor perhaps even the most significant reason, was the expansion of Islam into India.[209] Concluding that Islam's expansion into India was the reason for Buddhism's decline, some maintain, is a reductive fallacy which David Hackett Fischer in *Historians' Fallacies* explains, "reduces complexity to simplicity, or diversity to uniformity, in causal explanations."[210]

---

[208] Lao-Tse, "The Tao Teh King or The Tao and its Characteristics," part I, chap. 1-4.

[209] Gail Omvedt, *Buddhism in India: Challenging Brahmanism and Caste* (New Delhi: Sage Publications, 2003), 149, 150-165, 175-183.

[210] He continues with, "As long as historians tell selected truths, their causal models must be reductive in some degree. But some causal models are more reductive than others. When a causal model is reductive in such a degree, or in such a way, that the resultant distortion is dysfunctional to the resolution of the causal problem at hand, then the reductive fallacy is committed. One common form of the reductive fallacy is the confusion of necessary with sufficient cause – the confusion of causal

Fischer, though, goes on to acknowledge that this manner of reduction cannot "be entirely avoided in any historical interpretation," [211] since it is impossible to include every factor that helped to bring about a historical event. A factor other than Islamic invasion of India and the destruction of Buddhist temples in India by the invaders is that Buddhism rejected the caste system of Hinduism that was deeply rooted in the Indian psyche. Finally, since Buddhism came after Hinduism, it lacked the wealthy benefactors that Hinduism had acquired over its many years of existence.[212]

---

component without which an effect will not occur, with all the other causal components which are required to make it occur. This sort of error appears in causal explanations which are constructed like a single chain and stretched taught over a vast chasm of complexity." David Hackett Fischer, *Historians' Fallacies: Toward a Logic of Historical Thought* (New York: Harper & Row, 1970), 172.

[211] He continues with, "As long as historians tell selected truths, their causal models must be reductive in some degree. But some causal models are more reductive than others. When a causal model is reductive in such a degree, or in such a way, that the resultant distortion is dysfunctional to the resolution of the causal problem at hand, then the reductive fallacy is committed. One common form of the reductive fallacy is the confusion of necessary with sufficient cause – the confusion of causal component without which an effect will not occur, with all the other causal components which are required to make it occur. This sort of error appears in in causal explanations which are constructed like a single chain and stretched taught over a vast chasm of complexity." David Hackett Fischer, *Historians' Fallacies: Toward a Logic of Historical Thought* (New York: Harper & Row, 1970), 172.

[212] Hardy, 204.

The steady growth of Buddhism in China was accompanied by a moderate transformation of doctrine and practices of Indian expressions of Buddhism. Specifically, the Daoist appreciation of nature, Confucian loyalty to family ties, Daoist emphasis on the personal, and one-to-one intimate transmission of teaching were assimilated by Buddhism while developing in China. A Buddhist school that acquired a distinctly Chinese color is Mahayana Ch'an Buddhism. Other Buddhist schools that grew in China include Pure Land, to which you have already been introduced, Huanyan, and Taintai.[213] In the last half of the 800s AD, Ch'an Buddhism and Pure Land became the dominant schools.[214] The Ch'an school claims that its founder is the Indian Buddhist Bodhidharma (c. 460-534 AD) who traveled to China.

Mahayana Ch'an Buddhism spread to other East-Asian countries. In Korea, it is known as Son Buddhism, and in Japan as Zen Buddhism. Vietnam also owes its Buddhist tradition largely to Chinese Mahayana Ch'an Buddhism.[215] During the 600s AD, various expressions of Ch'an Buddhism developed. The Northern School of Ch'an advocated gradual enlightenment. In contrast, the Southern School argued for sudden enlightenment.[216] Both expressions of Ch'an Buddhism understand meditation as central

---

[213] Hardy, 246-251.
[214] Damien Keown, *A Dictionary of Buddhism* (Oxford: Oxford University Press, 2003), 58.
[215] Keown, 145, 327.
[216] Hardy, 249.

to Buddhism in accordance with the definition of the word Ch'an, which means meditation school.²¹⁷

~ The *Budai* Buddha ~

In China this Buddha is also called the Laughing Buddha. It is a Chinese version of the *Maitreya* Buddha of the Future.²¹⁸

219

Han-shan (Cold Mountain)

The writings of the Chinese poet Han-shan well-reflect the synthesis between Daoism and Buddhism of Chinese Buddhism. His name Han-shan translates

---

²¹⁷ Keown, 52.
²¹⁸ Eckel, 30.
²¹⁹ 邰秉宥 from Changhua, Taiwan, "Maitreya Buddha near Beipu," photograph, https://commons.wikimedia.org/wiki/File%3ABuddha_Beipu.jpg, (accessed July 10, 2015).

into Cold Mountain. Some accounts, though, refer to him as Han-yen which means Cold Cliffs. As with his name it is not certain when he lived. Some scholars place him right before the T'ang Dynasty in the short-lived dynasty that preceded the T'ang Dynasty called the Sui Dynasty (c.605-618).[220] While pondering on his poetry below, try to determine which elements come from Daoism and which from Buddhism.

Poem 1

Whoever reads my poems
Must protect the purity in his mind.

Stinginess and greed must change into honesty day after day;
Flattery and deceit must *right now* become the upright!

Expel and banish, wipe out your bad karma;
Return to rely on, accept your true nature.

Today! You must attain the Buddha-body;
Quickly! Quickly! Treat this just like it's imperial law![221]

---

[220] Han-Shan, *The Poetry of Han-shan: A Complete, Annotated Translation of Cold Mountain*, trans. Robert G. Henricks (Albany: State University of New York Press, 1990), 3, 11.

[221] Han-Shan, 31.

Poem 31

Dark and obscure-the way to Han-shan;
Far apart-the shores of the cold mountain stream.

Chirp, chirp-constantly there are the birds;
Silent and still-in addition there are no men.

Whisper, whisper-the wind blows in my face;
Whirling and swirling – the snow piles up all around.

Day after day-I don't see the sun'
And year after year-I've known no spring.[222]

Poem 228

In person I see the top of T'ien-t'ai;
Alone in its height-standing above the common crowd.

Swayed by the wind, pines and bamboo sight in harmony;
When the moon shines, the ocean and tides incessantly roll.

Below I look out to the edge of green hills;
To discuss things profound, I have the white clouds.

---

[222] Han-Shan, 70.

My delight in the wilds agrees with these mountains and
Streams;
My original ambition-to admire fellow followers of the way.[223]

Poem Number 277

In front of a cliff, all alone I silently sit;
The round moon brightly beams in the sky.

The ten thousand forms, as vague shadows appear in its midst,
But that one wheel-fundamentally, there is nothing on which it shines.

Free, empty, unbounded-my soul in itself it is pure;
Embracing the Void, I penetrate the mysterious and profound.

By using a finger we see the moon;
The moon is the hinge of the mind.[224]

Zen Buddhism

Buddhism was introduced into Japan during the early 500s AD. At the time the dominant way of worship in Japan was Shinto. Shinto believed in many

---

[223] Han-Shan, 314.
[224] Han-Shan, 19.

gods, with the sun Goddess Amaterasu as the central deity. For this reason Japan identifies itself with the land of the rising sun.[225]

Rising Sun Flag of Imperial Japan (1868–1947)[226]

After a brief period of tension between Shinto and Buddhism, the Japanese Prince Shotoku (573-621) affirmed Buddhism as a religion compatible with Shinto. According to Eckel, articles one and two of the *Seventeen Article Constitution of Japan* attributed to Prince Shotoku indicate that Shotoku promoted Buddhism in order to unify Japan politically.

---

[225] Eckel, 56.

[226] "Naval ensign of the Empire of Japan," design, https://commons.wikimedia.org/wiki/File%3ANaval_ensign_of_the_Empire_of_Japan.svg (accessed July 11, 2015).

~ Article Two of the Seventeen Article Constitution of Japan ~

Article 1

Harmony is to be valued, and an avoidance of wanton opposition to be honoured. All men are influenced by class-feelings, and there are few who are intelligent. Hence there are some who disobey their lords and fathers, or who maintain feuds with the neighbouring villages. But when those above are harmonious and those below are friendly, and there is concord in the discussion of business, right views of things spontaneously gain acceptance. Then what is there which cannot be accomplished!

Article 2

Sincerely reverence the three treasures. The three treasures, viz. Buddha, the law and the priesthood, are the final refuge of the four generated beings, and are the supreme objects of faith in all countries. What man in what age can fail to reverence this law? Few men are utterly bad. They may be taught to follow it. But if they do not betake them to the three treasures, how shall their crookedness be made straight?[227]

---

[227] http://www.duhaime.org/LawMuseum/lawarticle-1182/604-the-seventeen-article-constitution-of-japan.aspx (accessed July 11, 2015).

As a result of Prince Shotoku's support of Buddhism, a number of Japanese Buddhist schools took form including the following: Shingon, Tendai, Japanese Pure Land, and Zen Buddhism. Since Zen Buddhism is so well-known, we will focus on this popular school, which is the Japanese version of the Mahayana Chinese Ch'an School.[228] A principle proponent of Zen Buddhism was Dogen (1200-1253). Dogen made the practice of meditation even more central in Zen. Dogen also encouraged Zen Buddhism to fully embrace the doctrine of emptiness from Mahayana Buddhism that the Buddhist Indian Mahayana philosopher Nagarjuna (c. 150-250 AD) brought to the fore.[229] Below is a teaching of Dogen in which he stresses the importance of meditating in order to achieve emptiness.

~ Actualizing the Fundamental Point ~

To study the Buddha way is to study the self. To study the self is to forget the self. To forget the self is to be actualized by myriad things. When actualized by myriad things, your body and mind as well as the bodies and minds of others drop away. No trace of realization remains, and this no-trace continues endlessly.

When you first seek dharma, you imagine you are far away from its environs. But dharma is already

---

[228] Eckel, 56-64.
[229] Eckel, 61-62.

correctly transmitted; you are immediately your original self. When you ride in a boat and watch the shore, you might assume that the shore is moving. But when you keep your eyes closely on the boat, you can see that the boat moves. Similarly, if you examine myriad things with a confused body and mind you might suppose that your mind and nature are permanent. When you practice intimately and return to where you are, it will be clear that nothing at all has unchanging self.[230]

Zen Buddhism with its emphasis on nothingness brings out with great clarity a central difference between Buddhism and Judeo-Christian beliefs. According to Genesis, God created out of nothing (*creatio ex nihilo*). In other words, out of physical nothingness, God created something. The belief in God as a creator is central to Judaism and Christianity. This belief informs all other teachings and practices. One practical effect is the great value of being creative since we are made in the image and likeness of God who is the Creator. Zen Buddhism is almost like a reverse image of this central Judeo-Christian belief in creation. According to Zen Buddhism the physical world of suffering, the Wheel of Samsara, has always been. In order to escape this

---

[230] "Actualizing the Fundamental Point, the Genjo-koan," trans. Robert Aitken and Kazuaki Tanahashi, The Zen Site, http://www.thezensite.com/ZenTeachings/Dogen_Teachings/GenjoKoan_Aitken.htm, (accessed July 11, 2015).

eternal, timeless wheel of suffering, Buddha proposed attaining nothingness out of something.[231]

Quiz 9 for Chapter 9

1-5. As discussed in chapter eight, name and describe five prominent aspects of Daoism.

   1.

   2.

   3.

   4.

   5.

6-8. Explain the following terms in relationship to one another: *yin*, *yang*, and *qi*.

   6.

   7.

   8.

9-11. Identify and explain how one central Daoist principle is in continuity with Buddhism, and how two

---

[231] Eckel, 17.

other Chinese values, as explained in the chapter, helped to create a distinctly Chinese form of Buddhism.

9.

10.

11.

12-14. Explain how the Zen Buddhist value of emptiness and nothingness is in tension (or if you wish even contradicts) the Catholic teaching of *creatio ex nihilo*. For extra credit (3 points), also contrast the Zen emptiness and nothingness with the Catholic teaching of *creatio continua*.

Chapter 10: Confucius and Confucianism

Introduction

The Daoist-Buddhist synthesis competed with another synthesis that was dominant during China's Han Dynasty (206 BC-220 AD). This synthesis is called Han Confucianism. In contrast with Daoist and Buddhist thought, the political-philosophical synthesis of Han Confucianism valued family, scholarship, conformity to a moral code, actively fulfilling social duty, and submission to order established by the social hierarchy.[232] These Han-Confucian values are in tension with the Daoist-Buddhist emphasis on feminine attributes, governmental non-intervention, the personal, the spontaneous, emptiness and inaction. In studying Confucianism, we will begin with Confucius before turning our attention to key elements of his

---

[232] Grant Hardy, *Great Minds of the Eastern Intellectual Tradition*, Lectures 1-18 (Chantilly: The Great Courses, 2011), 99; Malcolm David Eckel, *Great World Religions: Buddhism*, Course Guidebook (Chantilly: Great Courses, 2003), 49.

philosophy.

Confucius

The Chinese philosopher Confucius (c. 551-479 BC) was born into the period of time that Karl Jaspers names the Axial Age. According to Jaspers, the Axial Age began in the 700s BC and lasted into the 200s BC. The Hebrew prophets, Siddhartha Buddha, Confucius, Founders of Hindu Vedic Schools, Zarathustra, Socrates, Aristotle, and Plato all lived during this pivotal age. According to Jaspers in *The Origin and Goal of History*:

~ The Axial Age ~

It would seem that this axis of history is to be found in the period around 500 B.C., in the spiritual process that occurred between 800 and 200 B.C. It is there that we meet with the most deep cut dividing line in history. Man, as we know him today, came into being. For short we may style this the 'Axial Period.'

The most extraordinary events are concentrated in this period. Confucius and Lao Tse were living in China, all the schools of Chinese philosophy came into being, including Mo-ti, Chuang-tse, Lieh-tsu, and a host of others; India produced Upanishads and Buddha and, like China, ran the whole gamut of philosophical possibilities down to skepticism, to materialism, sophism and nihilism; in Iran

Zarathustra taught a challenging view of the world as struggle between good and evil; in Palestine prophets made their appearance, from Elijah, by way of Isaiah and Jeremiah to Deutero-Isaiah; Greece witnessed the appearance of Homer, of the philosophers-Parmenides, Heraclitus and Plato-of the tragedians, Thucydides and Archimedes. Everything implied in these names developed during these few centuries almost simultaneously in China, India, and the West, without anyone of these regions knowing the others.[233]

Is Jasper's Axial Age compatible with the Christian teaching from Galatians chapter four verse four that Christ was sent in the "fullness of time"? I think it is possible as long as we see the Axial Age and its many profound thinkers preparing history with their pivotal thought for the Christian fullness of time. Confucius added to the collective wisdom of the Axial Age with his methodical approach to obtaining order in society. For Confucius, family, scholarship, and civic duty are to be at the service of a well-functioning state in which every person conforms to his role. The principle source of Confucius' teaching are the *Analects*. The *Analects* are a compilation of Confucian teachings by his students since he did not write down what he taught. Below are key excerpts of prominent Confucian values. Aspects of Confucian thought on

---

[233] Eugene Halton, *From the Axial Age to the Moral Revolution: John Stuart-Glennie, Karl Jaspers and the New Understanding of the Idea* (New York: Palgrave MacMillan, 2014), 2.

which we will focus our attention are the following: family, scholarship, conformity, and active civic duty.

Family

In the selections below from the *Analects,* Master Confucius and his disciples affirm filial piety. This entails reverence for one's ancestors that was officially sanctioned by the Shang Dynasty (c. 1600-1045 BC). When one's parents are alive, staying close to home is required by Confucius. Unlike his contemporary Siddhartha Buddha, who separated from his family in order to obtain enlightenment, Confucius never encourages such a radical detachment. Rather, Confucius teaches his followers to remain imbedded and loyal to their family, village, and nation.[234] For Confucius, personal identity is not defined by separation from community but rather defined by it, by the network of relationships that tie us together.[235]

Book I

CHAP. VI. The Master said, 'A youth, when at home, should be filial, and, abroad, respectful to his elders. He should be earnest and truthful. He should overflow in love to all, and cultivate the friendship of the good. When he has time and opportunity, after the performance of these things, he should employ them in polite studies.' CHAP.

---

[234] Eckel, 50.
[235] Hardy, 272.

VII. Tsze-hsia said, 'If a man withdraws his mind from the love of beauty, and applies it as sincerely to the love of the virtuous; if, in serving his parents, he can exert his utmost strength; if, in serving his prince, he can devote his life; if, in his intercourse with his friends, his words are sincere: — although men say that he has not learned, I will certainly say that he has.'[236]

CHAP. IX. The philosopher Tsang said, 'Let there be a careful attention to perform the funeral rites to parents, and let them be followed when long gone with the ceremonies of sacrifice; — then the virtue of the people will resume its proper excellence.'[237]

Book II

CHAP. V. 1. Mang I asked what filial piety was. The Master said, 'It is not being disobedient.' 2. Soon after, as Fan Ch'ih was driving him, the Master told him, saying, 'Mang-sun asked me what filial piety was, and I answered him, — "not being disobedient."' 3. Fan Ch'ih said, 'What did you mean?' The Master replied, 'That parents, when alive, be served according to propriety; that, when dead,

---

[236] James Legge, "The Chinese Classics (Confucian Analects)", Project Gutenberg, http://www.gutenberg.org/cache/epub/3330/pg3330-images.html, (accessed July 17. 2015).
[237] Legge, "The Chinese Classics (Confucian Analects)" (accessed July 17. 2015).

they should be buried according to propriety; and that they should be sacrificed according to propriety.'[238]

Book IV

CHAP. XIX. The Master said, 'While his parents are alive, the son may not go abroad to a distance. [239]

Scholarship

Repeatedly, Confucius exalts the role of the scholar, grave in his manners, who prefers study over wealth and luxury. During the Han Dynasty (206 BC-220 AD), a civil service exam centering on Confucian texts was mandated. The Confucian civil service exam was required in China all the way into the 1900s during China's last imperial dynasty, the Qing Dynasty (1644-1912).[240]

Book I

CHAP. VIII. 1. The Master said, 'If the scholar be not grave, he will not call forth any veneration, and his learning will not be solid. [241]

---

[238] Legge, "The Chinese Classics (Confucian Analects)."
[239] Legge, "The Chinese Classics (Confucian Analects)."
[240] Hardy, 84; Ronnie L. Littlejohn, *Confucianism: An Introduction* (London: I.B. Tauris, 2011), 72-73.
[241] Legge, "The Chinese Classics (Confucian Analects)."

Book IV

CHAP. IX. The Master said, 'A scholar, whose mind is set on truth, and who is ashamed of bad clothes and bad food, is not fit to be discoursed with.'[242]

Book XIII

CHAP. XXVIII. Tsze-lu asked, saying, 'What qualities must a man possess to entitle him to be called a scholar?' The Master said, 'He must be thus, — earnest, urgent, and bland: — among his friends, earnest and urgent; among his brethren, bland.'[243]

Book XIV

CHAP. III. The Master said, 'The scholar who cherishes the love of comfort is not fit to be deemed a scholar.'[244]

Book XIX

CHAP. I. Tsze-chang said, 'The scholar, trained for public duty, seeing threatening danger, is prepared to sacrifice his life. When the opportunity of gain is presented to him, he thinks of righteousness. In sacrificing, his thoughts are reverential. In

---

[242] Legge, "The Chinese Classics (Confucian Analects)."
[243] Legge, "The Chinese Classics (Confucian Analects)."
[244] Legge, "The Chinese Classics (Confucian Analects)."

mourning, his thoughts are about the grief which he should feel. Such a man commands our approbation indeed.'[245]

Conformity

Unlike the Daoists, Confucius does not emphasize spontaneity and individual creative expression. Instead, he stresses conformity to societal norms and to one's role in the social hierarchy. Acceptance of one's place in society, thought Confucius, is key to ensuring social stability. Public shame for having dishonored one's place in society, defined by the individual family and other set of relationships, also helps bring about virtuous behavior and societal stability. According to the scholar Grant Hardy, due to Confucianism "China is a land of polite, face-saving excuses."[246] This politeness and desire to keep up good, social appearances even if it means not directly admitting error, is, thinks Hardy, traceable "to Confucius and his ideas of ritual, deference, and hierarchy."[247]

Book I

CHAP. II. 1. The philosopher Yu said, 'They are few who, being filial and fraternal, are fond of offending against their superiors. There have been none, who, not liking to offend against their

---

[245] Legge, "The Chinese Classics (Confucian Analects)."
[246] Hardy, 84.
[247] Hardy, 84.

superiors, have been fond of stirring up confusion. 2. 'The superior man bends his attention to what is radical.[248]

CHAP. III. 1. The Master said, 'If the people be led by laws, and uniformity sought to be given them by punishments, they will try to avoid the punishment, but have no sense of shame. 2. 'If they be led by virtue, and uniformity sought to be given them by the rules of propriety, they will have the sense of shame, and moreover will become good.'[249]

CHAP. VIII. 1. The Master said, 'If the scholar be not grave, he will not call forth any veneration, and his learning will not be solid. 2. 'Hold faithfulness and sincerity as first principles. 3. 'Have no friends not equal to yourself.[250]

Book II

CHAP. XIX. The Duke Ai asked, saying, 'What should be done in order to secure the submission of the people?' Confucius replied, 'Advance the upright and set aside the crooked, then the people will submit. Advance the crooked and set aside the upright, then the people will not submit.'[251]

---

[248] Legge, "The Chinese Classics (Confucian Analects)".
[249] Legge, "The Chinese Classics (Confucian Analects)".
[250] Legge, "The Chinese Classics (Confucian Analects)".
[251] Legge, "The Chinese Classics (Confucian Analects)".

Book XII

CHAP. XI. 1. The Duke Ching, of Ch'i, asked Confucius about government. 2. Confucius replied, 'There is government, when the prince is prince, and the minister is minister; when the father is father, and the son is son.'[252]

Action and Civic Duty

Once again, unlike Daoism, Confucius does not bring to the fore inaction, passivity and non-intervention. In contrast, he desires his followers to see civic action as an important duty they are to fulfill. This public service is to be performed virtuously. Resorting to deception and Machiavellian-like manipulation in order to retain political office and order in society is contrary to Confucian thought.

Book I

CHAP. X. 1. Tsze-ch'in asked Tsze-kung, saying, 'When our master comes to any country, he does not fail to learn all about its government. Does he ask his information? or is it given to him?' 2. Tsze-kung said, 'Our master is benign, upright, courteous, temperate, and complaisant, and thus he gets his information. The master's mode of asking information! — is it not different from that

---

[252] Legge, "The Chinese Classics (Confucian Analects)".

of other men? [253]

Book II

CHAP. I. The Master said, 'He who exercises government by means of his virtue may be compared to the north polar star, which keeps its place and all the stars turn towards it.' [254]

Book XIII

CHAP. I. 1. Tsze-lu asked about government. The Master said, 'Go before the people with your example, and be laborious in their affairs.' [255]

Quiz 10 for Chapter 10

1-6. Compare and contrast the Daoist-Buddhist synthesis with the preceding Han Confucianism. In doing so, point out at least one similarity and at least four differences. Finally, explain which you like better, or if both why, and if neither why not.

7-9. According to Karl Jaspers what is the Axial Age? Is Jasper's Axial Age compatible

---

[253] Legge, "The Chinese Classics (Confucian Analects)."
[254] Legge, "The Chinese Classics (Confucian Analects)."
[255] Legge, "The Chinese Classics (Confucian Analects)."

with the Christian teaching from Galatians chapter four verse four that Christ was sent in the "fullness of time"? Why or why not?

10-12. Contrast Confucianism with Siddhartha Buddha's separation from his family. In addition, while keeping on this topic, contrast Christian teaching with Confucianism and Buddhism.

13. Explain, according to Confucian thought, the role of virtue in the life of a politician, or civil servant.

Chapter 11: Confucian Schools and Reconciliation with Daoism

Introduction

As with all deep thinkers, Confucius's thought was further developed. Two main ways by which Confucianism developed was regarding human nature. Mencius (327-289 BC) and his school interpreted Confucian thought in an optimistic manner, especially with respect to human nature. For this reason, Mencius does not stress the role of law as much as Xunzi (300-210 BC) and his more legalistic Confucian school does. Another way in which Confucianism developed was not by forming a new school but rather by interacting with Daoism, a philosophical approach that is very different from Confucianism.[256]

---

[256] Grant Hardy, *Great Minds of the Eastern Intellectual Tradition*, Lectures 1-18 (Chantilly: The Teaching Company, 2011), 120-131, 221-236.

Mencius and Human Nature

> Now, if anyone were suddenly to see a child about to fall into a well, his mind would be filled with alarm, distress, pity and compassion. That he would react accordingly is not because he would hope to use the opportunity to ingratiate himself with the child's parents, nor because he would hate the adverse reputation [that could come from not reacting accordingly]. From this it may be seen that one who lacks a mind that feels pity and compassion would not be human; one who lacks a mind that feels shame and aversion would not be human; one who lacks a mind that feels modesty and compliance would not be human; and one who lacks a mind that knows right and wrong would not be human.[257]

Mencius continues by identifying four good impulses as natural as having "four limbs." If these impulses are unimpeded, then good actions will result, or "sprout" forth as a flower sprouts from a bud. The first impulse is pity and compassion. The second impulse is "shame and aversion." The third impulse is "modesty and compliance," and the fourth impulse is the "sense of right and wrong."[258]

Pity and compassion flowers into humanness (*ren*), as his story about the child falling into a well illustrates. Shame and aversion blossoms into

---

[257] Mencius, *Mencius*, trans. Irene Bloom (New York: Columbia University Press, 2009), 35.
[258] Mencius, 35.

rightness (*yi*). Modesty and compliance grows into conforming to customs (propriety or *li*), and the sense of right and wrong is expressed by wisdom (*zhi*).[259]

Natural Impulses	Fruit of Natural Impulses
Pity/Compassion	Humanness (*ren*)
Shame/Aversion	Rightness (*yi*)
Modesty/Compliance	Propriety (*li*)
Sense of Right and Wrong	Wisdom (*zhi*)

According to Mencius, these impulses and fruits that define human nature are present in every human being. He states, "The goodness of human nature is like the downward course of water. There is no human being lacking in the tendency to do good, just as there is no water lacking in the tendency to flow downward."[260] To the objection that there are countless examples of people acting in ways contrary to his proposed natural feelings of compassion and modesty, Mencius argues that only when people are forced to do something contrary to their good impulses are bad actions done. Again with reference to water he explains, "by striking water and splashing it, you may cause it to go over your head, and by damming and channeling it, you may force it to flow uphill. But is this the nature of water? It is force that makes this happen. While people can be made to do what is not

---

[259] Mencius, 35.
[260] Mencius, 121.

good, what happens to their nature is like this."²⁶¹

This violence, further explains Mencius, may be defined in circumstances he calls "times of adversity." Adverse circumstances cause people to go against their natural tendencies to do good and avoid evil since, "In years of abundance, most of the young people have the wherewithal to be good, while in years of adversity, most of them become violent. This is not a matter of a difference in native capacities sent down by Heaven but rather of what overwhelms their minds."²⁶² Mencius also defines violence not merely by circumstances but also by choice, where people choose "to do violence to themselves." He asserts, "To deny propriety and rightness in one's speech is what is called 'doing violence to oneself.'"²⁶³

Mencius does not explain why people have a tendency to do violence to themselves in order to do evil rather than good. The Catholic explanation is that human beings are born with original sin that, even after baptism, leaves human nature with "an inclination to evil that is called 'concupiscence.'"²⁶⁴ This inclination does not mean, however, that human nature is intrinsically evil. Instead, the essential goodness of human nature is only wounded and deprived of original holiness and justice. Along with its natural inclination to goodness, human nature, according to the Catholic Church, is subject to

---

[261] Mencius, 121.
[262] Mencius, 125.
[263] Mencius, 79.
[264] *Catechism of the Catholic Church*, (Liguori: Liguori Publications, 1994), 405.

ignorance, suffering, and death.²⁶⁵

Xunzi and Human Nature

Contrary to Mencius, the Chinese Confucian scholar Xunzi held that human nature is naturally inclined to evil and not to good. According to Xunzi, "it is plain that human nature is evil and that any good in humans is acquired by conscious exertion."²⁶⁶ Being polite and well-mannered, such as a "son's deference to his father and a younger brother to his older brother," Xunzi asserts, "contradicts the true feelings inherent in his [man's] inborn nature."²⁶⁷

Unlike Mencius, who describes human nature like peaceful water that naturally flows into good actions, Xunzi compares human nature to a warped board. He states, "A straight board does not first need the press-frame to be straight; it is straight by nature. But a warped board must first await application of the press-frame, steam to soften it, and force to bend it into shape before it can be made straight; this is because by nature it is not straight."²⁶⁸ In order for the board, representing evil human nature, to be straight and, consequently, by definition good, Xunzi believes that a government of wise kings must impose

---

²⁶⁵ *Catechism of the Catholic Church*, (Liguori: Liguori Publications, 1994), 405.

²⁶⁶ Xunzi, *Xunzi: A Translation and Study of the Complete Works, Volume III, Books 17-32*, trans. John Knoblock (Stanford: Stanford University Press, 1994), 153.

²⁶⁷ Xunzi, 153.

²⁶⁸ Xunzi, 157.

morality and ritual on those below them. For this reason, Xunzi stresses the importance of law significantly more than Mencius does.[269] If law is not imposed in a forceful manner, argues Xunzi, then the supposedly most natural tendencies of human beings of greed, fighting, and "unrestrained passion" will be expressed.[270]

According to Catholicism, the violent, greedy, and unrestrained tendencies within human beings are not what is most essential to them. Neither original sin nor personal sin has erased men and women being made in the image and likeness of God who is good, all loving, and truthful. Since the goodness of human nature has been wounded by both original sin and by personal sins, men and women cannot, holds the Catholic Church, act fully in accordance with their essentially good natures. In order to do so, their intellects and will must, along with desires and emotions, cooperate with supernatural grace. Morality thus understood is not simply a matter of following emotions, as Mencius seems to indicate, or following the dictates of the will that corresponds to law imposed upon it externally, as Xunzi implies.[271]

Another critical difference between Catholicism and the Confucianism of both Mencius and Xunzi is the distinction the Catholic tradition makes between

---

[269] Xunzi, 157.

[270] Xunzi, 157-158.

[271] Peter Kreeft, *Practical Theology: Spiritual Direction form Saint Thomas Aquinas* (San Francisco: Ignatius Press, 2014), 110-111. Kreeft cites Thomas Aquinas's *Summa Theologica*, I-II, 58, 4).

guilt and shame. As explained by Peter Kreeft, relying upon St. Thomas Aquinas, in Catholicism "shame is social: being seen and disapproved by others. Guilt is individual: being seen and disapproved by God and/or your own conscience."[272] This distinction is made since, unlike Confucianism that is a socially-based ethics that may or may not acknowledge God's presence, in Catholicism God is central.

Confucianism: Mencius and Daoism

During China's Warring States (475-221 BC) and Qin Dynasty (221-206 BC), Xunzi's form of Confucianism dominated China. This meant that during these times the tendencies of human nature were automatically assumed as suspect and inclined to disorder, violence, and irrational behavior that could, if unchecked, lead to political instability. For this reason, law and harsh punishment, in particular in the Qin Dynasty, for those who broke laws were stressed.[273]

The long standing Han Dynasty (206 BC-220 AD) that followed the short lived Qin Dynasty embraced Mencius and his assumptions that since human nature is essentially good stressing law can be counter-productive. Mencius' form of Confucianism almost definitively replaced Xunzi's pessimistic

---

[272] Kreeft, 120. Kreeft cites Thomas Aquinas's *Summa Theologica*, I-II, 83, 1).

[273] Hardy, 130; Craig G. Benjamin, *Foundations of Eastern Civilization*, Lectures 1-24 (Chantilly: The Teaching Company, 2013), 160-176.

Confucianism after the Han Dynasty ended in part due to the teaching of the Chinese man, Ge Hong (283-343 AD).[274]

Ge Hong not only took a positive approach to Confucianism, in accordance with Mencius's interpretation, but also integrated Confucian teaching with Daoist belief in spontaneity, naturalism, individualism, and non-conformity.[275] The last characteristic of non-conformity may seem as completely incompatible with the repeated teachings of Confucius on conforming to societal norms. In his writings, Ge Hong dismisses this apparent contradiction by demonstrating how it is possible to be inwardly Daoist and outwardly, that is in public, Confucian.[276]

As observed by the scholar Grant Hardy, current Asian cultures influenced by a blend of Confucianism, and Daoist-Buddhism, especially China, strongly value Confucian elements of filial piety, paternalism, strong families, hierarchy, communities, conformity to societal norms, consensus, ritual, deference, along with more Daoist/Buddhist values of harmony, love of nature, and spontaneity within intimate settings.[277] The Western appreciation of individual autonomy, consequently, is significantly less valued in such Asian countries which understand a person's identity as derived from their community relationships.[278] Finally, the common, but not universal, Western way

---

[274] Hardy, 130, 226-236.
[275] Hardy, 130, 221.
[276] Hardy, 236.
[277] Hardy, 266, 278.
[278] Hardy, 272.

of directly stating one's faults and feelings is not, explains Hardy, pronounced in Asian countries whose cultures are steeped in Confucianism and Daoist-Buddhism. These Asian countries have been profoundly influenced by Confucian understanding of "ritual, deference and hierarchy" along with the Daoist-Buddhist value of harmony.[279] In relating his experience as a Westerner of a Chinese Asian view, strongly influenced by Confucianism and Daoism, Grant states:

> Harder to understand were the times when we made appointments to see people, and then they were deliberately not at home when we came back at the specified day and hour. They hadn't really wanted to continue the conversation, but it would've been rude to say so directly that would've made us "lose face" – and that's a really important concept that has to do with a person's dignity, and social status, and public persona. Sometimes when we'd knock on a door and people would open it and see us and then say oh please won't you come in even as they were shutting the door, they have to say come in even if they don't really want you to. It's not just what said, but it's how it's said. China is a land of polite, face-saving excuses. Eventually, I learned to do this as well. Once I forgot to go to an appointment and when I asked my more culturally-savvy associate what we should do, he said, "We're going to tell them we got sick." That's

---

[279] Hardy, 265-266.

not true, I said. He explained, "If we tell them we got sick, they'll figure that we forgot; if we tell them we forgot, they'll suspect that we didn't want to talk to them at all." "Ah" I said.[280]

Quiz 11 for Chapter 11

1-4. Compare and contrast Mencius and Xunzi on human nature. In doing so use the similes of water and a board.

5-9. How does the Catholic teaching on human nature differ from Mencius's? Include in your answer sin, intellect, will, emotions, and grace.

6-10. How does the Catholic teaching on human nature differ from Xunzi's? Include in your answer sin, intellect, will, emotions, and grace.

---

[280] Hardy, 265-266.

11-12. How does the Catholic understanding of shame and guilt differ from the teaching on shame in Confucian writing?

13. According to Ge Hong, how is it possible to be both a Daoist and a Confucian?

14-17. Comment on the following experience of Grant Hardy. What are the historical roots that he identifies for bringing about the supposedly distinctive Chinese, Asian cultural features he describes? Do you think he is correct? Why or why not?

> Harder to understand were the times when we made appointments to see people, and then they were deliberately not at home when we came back at the specified day and hour. They hadn't really wanted to continue the conversation, but it would've been rude to say so directly that would've made us "lose face" – and that's a really important concept that has to do with a person's dignity, and social status, and public persona. Sometimes when we'd knock on a door and people would open it and see us and then say oh please won't you come

in even as they were shutting the door, they have to say come in even if they don't really want you to. It's not just what said, but it's how it's said. China is a land of polite, face-saving excuses. Eventually, I learned to do this as well. Once I forgot to go to an appointment and when I asked my more culturally-savvy associate what we should do, he said, "We're going to tell them we got sick." That's not true, I said. He explained, "If we tell them we got sick, they'll figure that we forgot; if we tell them we forgot, they'll suspect that we didn't want to talk to them at all." "Ah" I said.[281]

---

[281] Hardy, 265-266.

Chapter 12: Legalism

Introduction

One way western students have memorized the dynasties of China is by singing them to the *Frere Jacques* tune. Try singing the dynasties to the following tune. Substitute the following Chinese names for the French words: Shang, Zhou, Qin, Han, Shang, Zhou, Qin, Han, Sui, Tang, Song, Sui, Tang, Song, Yuan, Ming, Qing, Republic, Yuan, Ming, Qing, Republic, Mao Ze Dong, Mao Ze Dong.

I bring the dynasties up in order to better aid you in locating our final topic of Legalism in Asian thought. Legalism is considered the third founda-

---

[282] Mysid, "Frère Jacques," sheet music, https://upload.wikimedia.org/wikipedia/commons/3/37/Fr%C3%A8re_Jacques.svg, (accessed August 3, 2015).

tional philosophy of China. The other two are Confucianism and Daoism. Legalism gained prominence during the Warring States Period (480-256 BC) which took place within last part of the Zhou Dynasty. The Zhou Dynasty came to a violent end when the Qin State seized power once they definitively overthrew the Zhou king.[283]

Legalism reached its apex of influence during the short lived Qin Dynasty (221-206 BC). The Qin dynasty preceded the Han dynasty in which Confucianism and Daoism were adopted. We will examine the ideology of Legalism from the perspective of the Qin ruler, Lord Shang (d. 338 BC) and through the philosophy of the anti-Confucian Han Feizi (d. 233 BC).[284]

Lord Shang and Legalism

Lord Shang (c. 390-338 BC) was a high office holder of the Qin State during the Warring States Period. The Legalist *Book of Lord Shang* is attributed to him.[285] As the following excerpts indicate, Lord Shang believed punishments need to be harsh and

---

[283] Craig G. Benjamin, *Foundations of Eastern Civilization*, Lectures 1-24 (Chantilly: The Great Courses, 2013), 92-98.

[284] Patricia Ebrey, Anne Walthall, and James Palais, *East Asia: A Cultural, Social, and Political History* (Belmont: Wadsworth, 2009), 31.

[285] Yang Shang, *The Book of Lord Shang: A Classic of the Chinese School of Law*, trans. Jan Julius Lodewijk Duyvendak (New Jersey: The Lawbook Exchange, 2009), viii.

rewards light, laws need to be clear, rulers need to be capable in applying the law and not necessarily the most intelligent, and power is to be concentrated in the ruler. In addition, the people, in their weakened political state, are to serve their country only by farming and by military service. Other disciplines are to be ignored including, history, rites, music, and the cultivation of virtue.

~ Lord Shang on Punishment ~

If penalties are made heavy and relations are involved in the punishments, petty and irascible people will not quarrel, intractable and stubborn people will not litigate, slothful and lazy people will not idle, those who waste their substance will not thrive, and those of evil heart, given to flattery, will bring about no change. If these five kinds of people do not appear within the territory, then it is certain waste lands will be brought under cultivation.[286]

If penalties are made heavy and rewards light, the ruler loves his people and they will die for him; but if rewards are made heavy and penalties light, the ruler does not love his people, nor will they die for him. When, in a prosperous country, penalties are applied, the people will reap profit and at the same time stand in awe; when rewards are applied, the

---

[286] Shang, "The Book of Lord Shang," Order to Cultivate Waste, no. 11.

people will reap profit and at the same time have love.[287]

Punishment produces force, force produces strength, strength produces awe, awe produces virtue. Virtue has its origin in punishments. For the more punishments there are, the more valued are rewards, and the fewer rewards there are, the more heed is paid to punishments, by virtue of the fact that people have desires and dislikes.[288]

~ Lord Shang on Clarity of Law and the Law Giver ~

The way to administer a country well, is for the law for the officials to be clear; therefore one does not rely on intelligent and thoughtful men. The ruler makes the people single-minded, and therefore they will not scheme for selfish profit. Then the strength of the country will be consolidated. A country where the strength has been consolidated, is powerful, but a country that loves talking is dismembered.

The way in which a sage administers a state is by unifying rewards, unifying punishments, and unifying education. The effect of unifying rewards is that the army will have no equal; the effect of unifying punishments is that orders will be carried

---

[287] Shang, "The Book of Lord Shang," Elimination of Strength, no. 4.
[288] Shang, "The Book of Lord Shang," Discussion about the People, no. 8.

out; the effect of unifying education is that inferiors will obey superiors. Now if one understands rewards, there should be no expense; if one understands punishments, there should be no death penalty; if one understands education, there should be no changes, and so people would know the business of the people and there would be no divergent customs. The climax in the understanding of rewards is to bring about a condition of having no rewards; the climax in the understanding of punishments is to bring about a condition of having no punishments; the climax in the understanding of education is to bring about a condition of having no education.[289]

~ Lord Shang on a Strong Government and Weak People ~

A weak people means a strong state and a strong state means a weak people. Therefore, a country, which has the right way, is concerned with weakening the people. If they are simple they become strong, and if they are licentious they become weak. Being weak, they are law-abiding; being licentious, they let their ambition go too far; being weak, they are serviceable, but if they let their ambition go too far, they will become strong. Therefore is it said, "To remove the strong by means of a strong people brings weakness; to

---

[289] Shang, "The Book of Lord Shang," Rewards and Punishments, no. 1.

remove the strong by means of a weak people brings strength."[290]

~ Lord Shang on Farming and Military Service ~

Therefore is it said: If there are a thousand people engaged in agriculture and war, and only one in the Odes and History, and clever sophistry, then those thousand will all be remiss in agriculture and war; if there are a hundred people engaged in agriculture and war and only one in the arts and crafts, then those hundred will all be remiss in agriculture and war.[291]

The country depends on agriculture and war for its peace, and likewise the ruler, for his honor. Indeed, if the people are not engaged in agriculture and war, it means that the ruler loves words and that the officials have lost consistency of conduct. If there is consistency of conduct in officials, the country is well-governed; and if single-mindedness is striven after, the country is rich; to have the country both rich and well governed is the way to attain supremacy. Therefore is it said, "The way to supremacy is no other than by creating single-mindedness!"[292]

---

[290] Shang, "The Book of Lord Shang," Weakening the People, no. 1.
[291] Shang, "The Book of Lord Shang," Agriculture and War, no. 4.
[292] Shang, "The Book of Lord Shang," Agriculture and War, no. 4.

If, in a country, there are the following ten things: odes and history, rites and music, virtue and the cultivation thereof, benevolence and integrity, sophistry and intelligence, then the ruler has no one whom he can employ for defense and warfare. If a country is governed by means of these ten things, it will be dismembered as soon as an enemy approaches, and even if no enemy approaches, it will be poor. But if a country banishes these ten things, enemies will not dare to approach, and even if they should, they would be driven back. When it mobilizes its army and attacks, it will gain victories; when it holds the army in reserve and does not attack, it will be rich. A country that loves strength makes assaults with what is difficult, and thus it will be successful. A country that loves sophistry makes assaults with what is easy, and thus it will be in danger. Therefore sages and intelligent princes are what they are, not because they are able to go to the bottom of all things, but because they understand what is essential in all things. Therefore the secret of their administration of the country lies in nothing else than in their examination of what is essential.[293]

Han Feizi and Confucian Virtue

The philosopher Han Feizi (c. 280-233 BC)

---

[293] Shang, "The Book of Lord Shang," Agriculture and War, no. 5.

studied under the Confucian Xunzi. In time, Han Feizi rejected the Confucianism of his teacher. Han Feizi thought the Confucian belief that effective governments need to be virtue based is impractical and foolish. In accordance with Xunzi's pessimistic view of human nature, Han Feizi held that since human nature is intrinsically selfish, rulers should not exhibit warmth to their subjects nor reveal their thoughts and plans to them.

Instead, in this state of unknowing, the ideal ruler, is to foster rivalry among his subjects in order to manipulate them for his own purposes and the good of the state. One way Feizi encouraged deceitful manipulation was by taking credit for success and blaming failures on his subordinates.[294] Agreeing with Lord Shang, Han Feizi also believed laws and punishments need to be clear. Clarity of law, argued Han Feizi, will allow people to determine with clarity that it is in their self-interest to keep the law in order to avoid punishment. [295]

~ Han Feizi on Strong Law and a Strong State ~

No state is forever strong or forever weak. If those who uphold the law are strong, the state will be

---

[294] Hardy, 142.
[295] Ebrey, Walthall, and Palais, 31; Han Feizi, *Han Feizi: Basic Writings*, trans. Burton Watson (New York: Columbia University Press, 2003), 10.

strong; if they are weak, the state will be weak.[296]

~ Han Feizi on Rulers Cautiously Staying in the Background While Maintaining Clear and Strong Laws ~

When each exercises his ability, the ruler need do nothing. If the ruler tries to excel, then nothing will go right. If he boasts of an eye for the abilities of others, he will invite deceit among his subordinates.[297]

~ Han Feizi on Non-Lenient Rulers ~

If he is lenient and fond of sparing lives, his subordinates will impose upon his kind nature.[298]

~ Han Feizi on a Strict Hierarchy ~

If the superior and inferior try to change roles, the state will never be ordered. Use the single Way and make names the head of it. When names are correct, things stay in place; when names are twisted, things shift about. Hence the sage holds to unity in stillness; he lets names define themselves and affairs reach their own settlement.[299]

~ Han Feizi on Rulers not Revealing their Natures ~

---

[296] Feizi, 21.
[297] Feizi, 36.
[298] Feizi, 36.
[299] Feizi, 36.

He [the ruler] does not reveal his nature, and his subordinates are open and upright. He assigns them tasks according to their ability and lets them settle things for themselves; he hands out rewards according to the results and lets them raise their own station. He establishes the standard, abides by it, and lets all things settle themselves. On the basis of names he makes his appointments, and where the name is not clear, he looks to the actual achievement it applies to. According to how achievement and name tally, he dispenses the reward and punishment deserved. When rewards and punishments are certain to be handed out, then subordinates will bare their true nature.[300]

With respect to maintaining a strict sense of hierarchy, how does Han Feizi's teaching differ from Jesus' insistence in Mark chapter ten verse forty-four that "whoever wishes to be first among you shall be slave of all"? (NAB) Jesus shocked Peter by fulfilling his teaching when he stooped to wash the feet of his disciples:

Now before the festival of the Passover, Jesus knew that his hour had come to depart from this world and go to the Father. Having loved his own who were in the world, he loved them to the end. 2 The devil had already put it into the heart of Judas son of Simon Iscariot to betray him. And during supper 3 Jesus, knowing that the Father had given

---

[300] Feizi, 36.

all things into his hands, and that he had come from God and was going to God, 4 got up from the table, took off his outer robe, and tied a towel around himself. 5 Then he poured water into a basin and began to wash the disciples' feet and to wipe them with the towel that was tied around him. 6 He came to Simon Peter, who said to him, "Lord, are you going to wash my feet?" 7 Jesus answered, "You do not know now what I am doing, but later you will understand." 8 Peter said to him, "You will never wash my feet." Jesus answered, "Unless I wash you, you have no share with me." 9 Simon Peter said to him, "Lord, not my feet only but also my hands and my head!" (John 13: 1-9 NRSV)

The writings of the great Catholic theologian St. Thomas Aquinas challenge Han Feizi's dismissal of virtue as central to politics. For Aquinas, influenced by Aristotle, the main purpose of political life is virtue and not only order and prosperity.[301] According to Aquinas, since man is social by nature it is natural for man to live in society, for only in the context of social living can human beings attain their natural end that is meant to be fulfilled supernaturally by grace in heaven. The ultimate end of political communities, therefore, is to seek "the supreme human good...the common good...which is superior to...the good of an

---

[301] Michael J. Sweeney, "Aquinas on Limits to Political Responsibility for Virtue: A Comparison to Al-Farabi," *The Review of Metaphysics* 62, no. 4 (June 2009): 819, 821.

individual."[302] This means that for Aquinas, the final end of the individual, the family, and the political state is to live virtuously and to attain eternal life.[303]

While acknowledging the great importance of the political realm, Aquinas affirms the family as a small community that is relatively autonomous from the political state. The family limits the responsibility politicians have in instilling civic virtue since much of this virtue formation, respecting the principle of subsidiarity, is meant to develop within each family unit.[304] Since along with the state the family is ordered to virtue, when a child becomes an adult the role of the state in a way replaces the role of the

---

[302] Thomas Aquinas, *Sententia libri Politicorum Commentary on Aristotle's Politics*, trans. Ernest L. Fortin and Peter D. O'Neill (Spiazzi, 1951) bk 1, lesson 1, Dominican House Priory, http://dhspriory.org/thomas/Politics.htm (accessed September 8, 2014).

[303] Thomas Aquinas, *De Regno*, trans. Gerald B. Phelan (Toronto: The Pontifical Institute of Mediaeval Studies, 1949), bk. I, chapter, 15, 107, Dominican House Priory, http://dhspriory.org/thomas/DeRegno.htm#15, (accessed September 20, 2014). "[107] Yet through virtuous living man is further ordained to a higher end, which consists in the enjoyment of God, as we have said above. Consequently, since society must have the same end as the individual man, it is not the ultimate end of an assembled multitude to live virtuously, but through virtuous living to attain to the possession of God."

[304] Sweeney, 824. Sweeny cites, Aquinas, *Commentary on Aristotle's Nicomachean Ethics*, Bk 10, lect. 15, n. 2159; Aquinas, *Commentary on Aristotle's Politics*, 1.1; Aquinas, *Scriptum super libros Sententiarum Magistri Petri Lombardi* bk. 4; Aquinas, *Summa Contra Gentiles* bk. 3, qq. 122-5, bk. 4. Q. 78; Aquinas, *Summa Theologica*, q. 41-68.

family. If the new adult has not internalized virtue when in his blessed state as a child within a family hopefully aided by sacramental grace, the state has the duty to coerce him to be virtuous when he commits public vices.[305] Similar to how Aquinas upholds the relative autonomy of a family from the state, he also upholds relative autonomy of other non-state institutions such as religious communities, guilds, and universities. All of these institutions also have some role that is distinct, but not absolutely, from the state with respect to virtue formation.[306]

Both Lord Shang and Han Feizi differ from Aquinas regarding what is most important. In the writings of Lord Shang and Han Feizi, a strong government that teaches clear and forceful laws is of utmost importance. Aquinas, while not necessarily disagreeing with this, teaches that a strong government that coercively enforces strong laws is not sufficient and, in a way is lower, to the more fundamental institution of the family. Aquinas is able to maintain this without contradiction since he upholds a political hierarchy, in which the state has precedence, with an ontological hierarchy in which the family, although lower in the political order, has precedence. Ontologically speaking, the family is greater than the political state since, among other aspects, it is meant to instill virtue by way of love and grace rather than by force and fear. The ontological

---

[305] Sweeney, 825.

[306] Sweeney, 829-830. Sweeny cites Aquinas, *Summa Theologica*, II-II, q. 40, a. 1, Aroney, "Subsidiarity, Federalism, and the Best Constitution," 197, n. 151.

and political hierarchies are not to be understood equivocally nor univocally but analogically.[307] Both the loving context of the family and the more coercive political realm need each other. The family needs the state since the family lacks the self-sufficiency that the state has. The political state needs the family since the family in its loving environment can more effectively encourage virtue than the state can.[308]

Quiz 12 for Chapter 12

1-3. List the three foundational philosophies of China.

1.

2.

3.

4. When was Legalism dominant in China?

5-8. What is the position of the Book of Lord Shang on punishment, rewards, power, and farming/military service?

---

[307] Sweeney, 832.
[308] Sweeney, 832.

9-10. What aspect did Han Feizi keep from his education under Xunzi? What aspect did he reject from Xunzi's Confucianism?

11-14. Describe Han Feizi's views on the ideal ruler. Include in your answer the following: unknowing state, law, rivalry, and manipulation.

15-17. From a Catholic perspective, briefly respond to Lord Shang's and Han Feizi's teachings.

Index

Amitabha 123, 124
Analects 161-169
anatta 113, 114, 116
Aquinas 44, 89, 177, 193-195
Aristotle 160, 193
Atman 27, 28, 31, 38, 39, 113, 116
Augustine 71-73, 118
Axial Age 160, 161

Benedict XVI 29, 31, 118
Bhagavad-gita 80, 81
bodhisattvas 119-123, 125
Brahman 26-28, 31, 32, 38-41, 64, 67, 82, 83, 85
Bronze Age 1, 5-7
Buddha 93, 95-98, 100-102, 107, 110-113, 117, 118, 121, 123-128, 148, 149, 153-155, 160, 162

caste system 26, 27, 146
Chan Buddhism 135, 145
Chinese rites 20
civic virtue 194
Confucius 9, 10, 14, 24, 135, 159-162, 164, 166-8, 171, 178

Dalai Lama 129-131
Dao 10, 139, 142, 144,
Daodejing 135, 136, 138, 139, 141
Daoism 9, 135, 141, 145, 148, 149, 168, 171, 177, 179, 184
Devi 85, 88
dharma 129, 131, 154

Ecumenical Council of Vienne 51
Eightfold Path 93, 99-101
Emptiness 116, 117, 136, 142, 144, 145, 154, 159

face-saving 166, 179
Feuerbach 88-89
Four Noble Truths 93, 98, 99
Fourth Lateran Council 44

Ge Hong 178

Han Dynasty 159, 164, 177, 178, 184
Han Feizi 9, 13, 14, 184, 189, 190-193, 195
Han-shan 148, 150
Hatha Yoga 49, 55
Hinayana 96, 116,
Humani Generis 2

infusion of a rational soul 4
Iron Age 1, 5, 8

Jainism 63, 64, 66, 67, 93
Jesuit missionaries 20
John Paul II 3, 97

Kali 85-87
Karl Jaspers 160
karma 27, 28, 50, 66, 130, 149
Krishna 81, 82

Laozi 9, 10, 135
Laughing Buddha 148
Lord Shang 184-188, 190, 195

Madhva 42-44
Mahadevi 85
Mahavira 63, 74, 93
Mahayana 96, 97, 107, 108, 110, 115, 116, 120-123, 128, 135, 147, 154
Manichaeism 63, 71
Matteo Ricci 20
Mencius 171-178
Middle Way 93, 96, 117
moksha 27, 28

Nagarjuna 116, 117, 154
Neolithic 1, 6
New Stone Age 5, 6
Nibbana 101, 107, 112
nirvana 96, 98, 100, 101, 103, 107, 108, 112, 117, 121-123

Old Stone Age 5
Old Wisdom School 96
oracle bones 6, 19, 24, 139

Paleolithic 1, 5
Pali 108, 112, 116
Patanjali 49, 52
Pius XII 2
Pre-history 1, 4

Prince Arjuna 80-82
Prince Shotoku 152, 153
Puranas 80, 82
Pure Land 122-124, 147, 153

Qin Dynasty 177, 184
Qing Dynasty 23, 164

Ramanuja 39, 40, 42, 43

Sakti 85
Samkhya 37, 49-52
samsara 27, 28, 117, 155
Shang dynasty 17-19, 22, 23, 162
Shangdi 20-21
Shankara 38, 39, 42, 43
Shinto 151, 152
Shiva 83-85
Siddhartha Gautama 93
Siva 85
subsidiarity 194

Tantric School 117
Tantrism 87
Tao Te Ching 10-12
Teresa of Avila 54
Theravada ... 102, 107, 108, 110, 112-116, 121-123, 128
Thuggees 87
Tibetan Buddhism 107, 108, 128, 131

Uddalaka 17, 32

Upanishads 17, 27, 28, 31, 38, 88, 160
Vajrayana 108
Vardamana 63
Vedanta 37-43, 49
Vedas 17, 25-27, 37-39, 63
Vishnu 79, 81, 83, 85

Warring States 24, 177, 184
Warring States Period 24, 184
William Sleeman 87

Xunzi 171, 175-178, 190

Yijing 17, 24, 25
yin and yang 139, 140
Yoga 37, 49, 52-56,
Yoga Sutras 53, 55

Zen Buddhism 135, 137, 151, 153-155,
Zhou Dynasty 17, 23, 24, 184
Zoroastrianism 63, 67, 71

www.ingramcontent.com/pod-product-compliance
Lightning Source LLC
Chambersburg PA
CBHW031317160426
43196CB00007B/574